Adobe Captivate 8 – Getting Creative

Advanced Techniques for Power Users

and

Creative Developers

Wayne Pascall

1

Adobe Captivate 8 – Getting Creative

Copyright © 2014 by Wayne Pascall

Table of Contents

3

Table of Contents

Table of Contents

INTENDED AUDIENCE FOR THIS BOOK

This book is intended for those who have already mastered the fundamentals on using Adobe Captivate 8. One of the best ways to learn is by doing and practice. The focus of this book is to master Captivate skills, especially the new features of Captivate 8, by working through exercises in creative projects. With clear step-by-step guidelines, you will be building interactive, reusable learning objects and learning to use the advanced tools of Captivate 8. These exercises are ideal for creative developers who would like to use Captivate beyond its normal uses or to add some flair to traditional projects.

- Use the new features in Captivate 8 that promote creativity

- Draw and paint a 3D digital piano right inside Captivate 8

- Draw and paint a 3D Mp3 player right inside Captivate 8

- Build a highly interactive digital piano

- Use Characters and Smart Shapes to create a Storytelling Scenario

- Edit a Captivate animation in Flash and use it in Captivate

- Edit a Captivate Certificate Widget in Flash and use it in Captivate

- Build varieties of charts using the Charts Widget

- Use Rollover Slidelets in an interactive Learning Object for American Sign Language

- Use text-to-speech in an interactive Learning Object for American Sign Language

- Use 508 Compliance in an interactive Learning Object for American Sign Language

- Use Variables and Advanced Actions to provide information each time an image is clicked

- Use Shared Advanced Actions

- Use Variables and Advanced Actions to disable navigation till all objects are clicked.

- Use Variables and Advanced Actions to personalize and customize courses based on a personality assessment

- Use Variables and Advanced Actions to personalize and customize courses based on a pretest and advanced quizzing

- Use Best Practices in Captivate 8 to complete projects efficiently with less rework

You can preview the sample projects at the Advanced Interactions page of the **elearnvisual.com** website. Use the directions at the end of each chapter to download the Captivate source files.

1 - New Features for Creativity

Here are some new features that will help you be creative in Captivate projects.

New Characters and Poses

There are new out-of-the-box assets, including 20 new characters, 50 different poses.

New Text-to-Speech Voices

In addition to "Paul" and "Kate", Captivate 8 is loaded with 4 additional text-to-speech voices. Here is the total list:

- **Kate**: English female voice
- **Paul**: English male voice
- **Bridget**: British English female voice
- **James**: British English female voice
- **Julie**: US English female voice
- **Chloe**: Canadian French female voice
- **Yumi**: Korean voice

New Color Swatches

Captivate 8 now allows you to access ready-made combinations of colors or swatches much like Photoshop. You can also create and load custom color palettes. This is an excellent addition to creative and artistic tasks in Captivate.

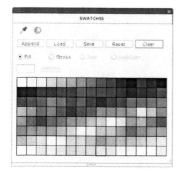

Enhanced Themes with New Theme Colors

Each of the 11 themes now has a set over 20 preset groups of colors. You can further customize these colors allowing for many variations in the theme colors. You can also import color swatches from Adobe Photoshop.

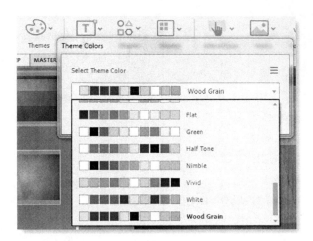

Advanced Actions and Variables Enhancements

You can now drag and drop shared actions from the library directly on to objects and parameterize variables.

There is now a preview button in the advanced actions pane. This button assists developers to see all elements in advanced action, especially if/then conditional actions that have multiple decisions and collapsed panes. You can now duplicate decisions and re-arrange their order.

Tracking variable usage

Now in the **Variables** dialog box, you can track the usage of variables in a project by clicking g the Usage button.

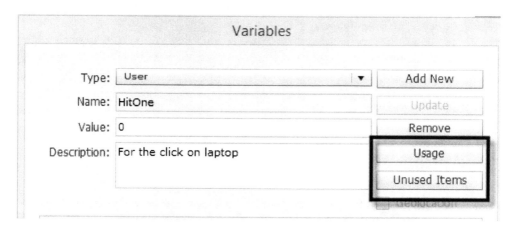

More Tools for Consistency

Lock Size and Position of Objects

In previous versions of Captivate, when you locked an object not only did you lock its position, but you could not edit its properties. In Captivate 8 there is another option where you can just lock the size and position of an object and still be able to edit it. This is a great feature for objects that you do not want to accidentally move and continue working on them.

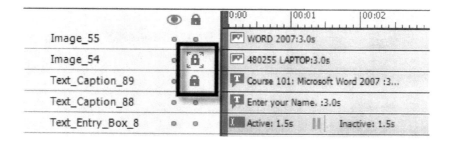

Smart Positioning of Objects

The Smart Position feature assists you in achieving consistency in the positioning of objects across the project and achieves consistency in position and display on mobile devices.

Actions for Controlling the Playbar and Table of Contents.

Previously in Captivate, to lock, hide the playbar or table of contents for a given slide, you had to manipulate system variables. Now these functions can simply be accessed from the list of actions. Toggle is also another available action for manipulating variables back and forth between 0 and 1. These two features make it a lot simpler to create certain advanced actions with less scripting.

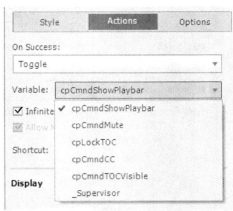

Smart Shapes Enhancements

Using Smart Shapes As Animated Buttons

Using Smart Shapes as buttons in Captivate has been enhanced so that the Smart Shapes behave like animated buttons with down and over states.

Save Smart Shapes as Free-Form Shapes

Now you can save and reload Smart Shapes that you have modified into free-form shapes. In addition, there is a Polygon Shape tool to assist you in creating new shapes.

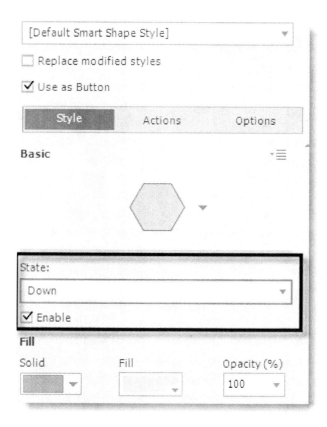

Adobe Captivate 8 allows you to define up, over and down states for Smart Shapes when using them as buttons.

Web Objects

You can now embed Web Objects into your projects, which could be a YouTube video or website.

HTML5 Animations

You can now import HTML5 and Edge Animations directly into Adobe Captivate. Position and resize the animations where you like and publish to HTML5 format. This presents lots of opportunities for enhanced interactivity beyond what can be created inside Captivate.

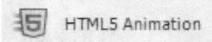

2 – POWER UP YOUR VISUAL DESIGN

Filters and Effects

With the graphic design features in Captivate 8 such as **gradients**, **drop shadows**, **reflections**, **bevel filters** and **smart shapes** it is now possible to create visually appealing graphics, diagrams, illustrations and quizzes without relying on an external program. In this chapter, we will be looking at how to create and edit drop shadows, create and edit gradients. We would also learn how to access and use quiz templates.

Drop Shadows

1. To add a **drop-shadow** to an object, first **click** the object, so that it is selected.

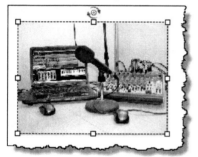

2. Open the **Shadow and Reflection** section of the Property Inspector and select a **preset** for a quick shadow type.

3. You can adjust the shadow by manipulating the properties for:

    A. **Percentage (%)**
    B. **Blur**
    C. **Angle**
    D. **Distance**
    E. **Color**

Gradients

Adding Gradients

1. To add a **gradient** to an object, first **click** the object, so that it is selected.

2. In the **Fill** section of the Property Inspector and click the **Fill** tool.

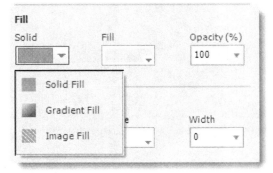

3. Click **Gradient Fill** in the window that launches.

4. Click the **Fill** tool and choose a **color** from the **top row** of colors that most closely matches the gradient you want to create. You can adjust this color later.

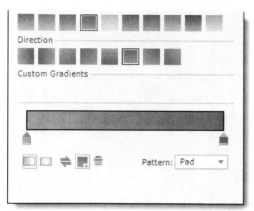

5. Choose a **Direction** from the **second row** that most closely matches the style of gradient you want to create. You can adjust this style later. This is a linear gradient.

6. Your object is filled with the selected gradient.

7. You can **customize gradients** by manipulating properties of:
   A. **Direction**
   B. **Colors**
   C. **Pattern**
   D. **Reverse Colors**
   E. **Radial Gradient**
   F. **Linear Gradient**
   G. **Alpha Setting**
You can then save your customized gradient as a preset.

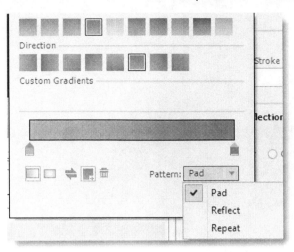

Customizing Gradients

We are going to create a radial gradient, with the colors red and yellow and save it as a preset.

1. To add a customized **gradient** to an object, first **click** the object, so that it is selected.

2. In the **Fill** section of the Property Inspector and click the **Fill** tool.

3. Click **Gradient Fill** in the window that launches.

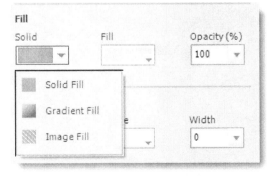

4. Click the **Fill** tool and choose a **color** from the **top row** of colors that most closely matches the gradient you want to create. You can adjust this color later.

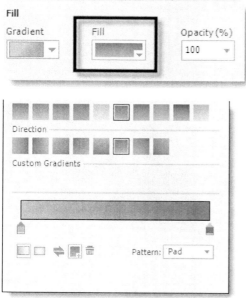

5. Click on the **Radial** tool to change the gradients to radial types.

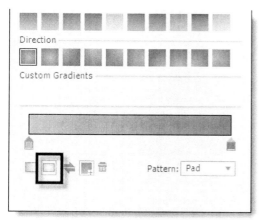

6. Clicking the **Color Stops** will launch the color palette. **Click** the **Color Stop** on the extreme right and choose a red color. You can specify the type of red more accurately by entering the appropriate hexadecimal numbers.

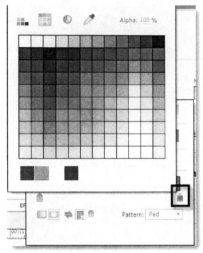

7. **Click** the **Color Stop** on the extreme left and choose a yellow color. You can specify the type of yellow more accurately by entering the appropriate hexadecimal numbers.

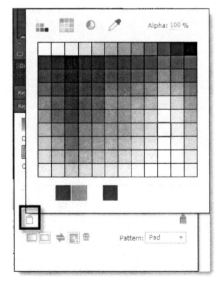

8. You can **add additional colors** to your gradient by positioning the cursor between Color Stops until a plus (+) sign appears, and then click to add an additional Color Stop.

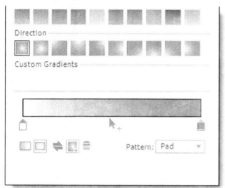

9. Click on the new **Color Stop** to add additional colors to the gradient. Follow the same procedure to add additional colors to linear gradients.

To **remove** colors from the gradient, click the stop color tool that corresponds to the color you want to remove and drag it **downwards** and **away** from the gradient slider.

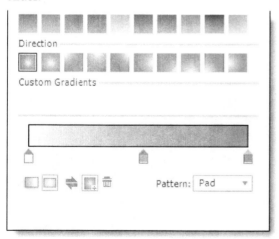

10. Click the **Add Custom Gradient** icon to add your custom gradient to the Custom Gradients list for reuse.

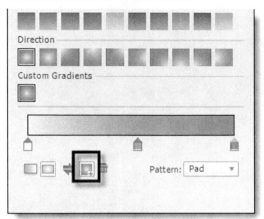

11. You can quickly reverse the colors of the gradient by clicking the **Reverse Colors** tool.

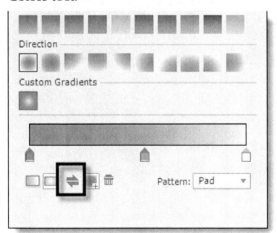

12. Your new **customized gradient** fill applied to a rectangle.

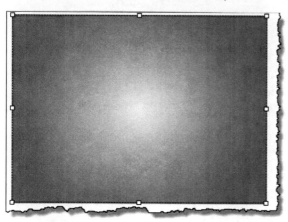

Editing Gradients

1. To edit a gradient, first click the object with the gradient fill, then right-click and select **Edit Gradient**, or click Edit > **Edit Gradient**.

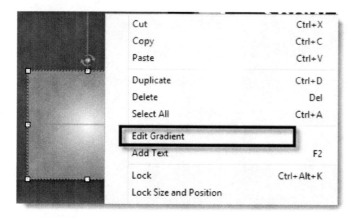

2. A **line** with a circular start point and a square end point appears inside your gradient. Changing the **angle** and **length** of this line gives you precise control over gradient you have just created.

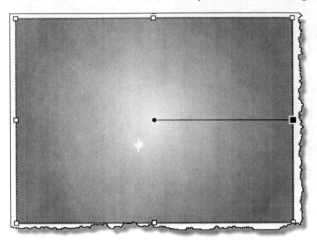

3. **Shortening** the length of the line causes the gradient to be distributed over a **smaller area**. Making the line longer will have the reverse effect.

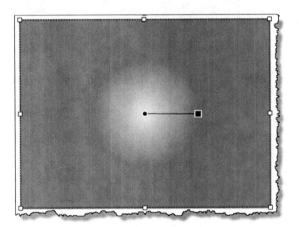

Adding Text to Gradients & Fills

1. Right-click the object with the gradient fill and select **Add Text**.

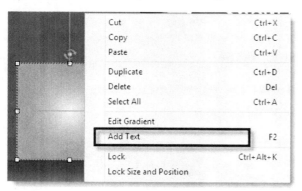

2. Add your desired text to the gradient. Customize the **format, size, color** and **alignment** of text from the **Character** tab in the Properties panel.

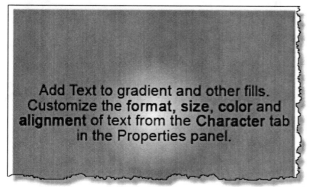

NEW: Using Color Swatches

This new feature in Captivate 8 gives you creative flexibility in adding colors to your objects. You can create a customized palette of colors for Fill, Stroke, Text and Highlight properties of objects. You can save and reload these customized color swatches and also import swatches from other programs like Photoshop.

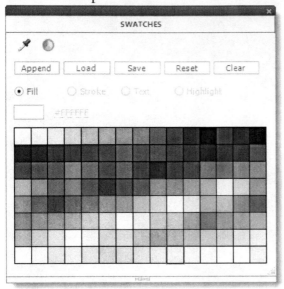

To load the Color Swatches panel:

- Click **Window** > **Swatches**

NOTE: To use the Swatch on a block of text or a shape, first select the text or shape, then click **Window** > **Swatches**

Creating a Customized Color Swatch

In this example, we will create a customized color swatch. The color swatch is part of a company's style guide which includes specifications for title texts. The color of the text needs to have an RGB (Red, Green, Blue) value of R-64, G-32 and B-94, or a hexadecimal value of -#40205E. We will create this color as part of the swatch.

1. Select the block of text on which you would like to apply the new color.

2. Click **Window** > **Swatches**

3. Click the **Color Picker** icon on the Swatches window

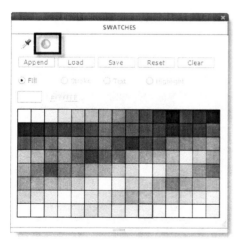

4. Enter the hexadecimal (#40205E) or RGB values for the desired color and click **OK**.

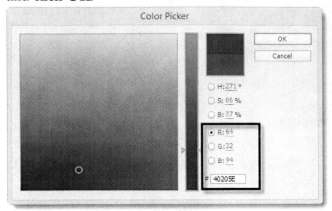

5. Enter a name for your new Swatch and click **OK**.

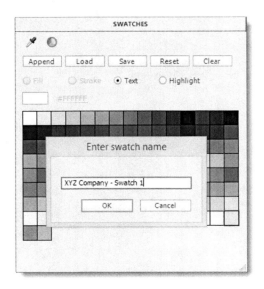

6. Your new color is added to the swatch.

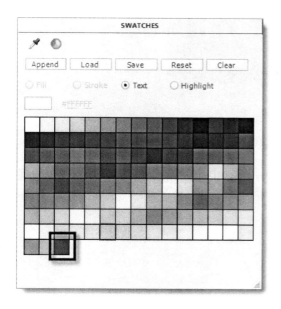

7. Click the **Save** button on the Swatches Window to save your swatch to a desired location.

8. Your text with the new color applied from your newly created Swatch.

9. Click **Load** on the Swatches window to load a saved Swatch and repeat the above steps to add more colors to your swatch. In this way, you can create a swatch or combination of swatches that are part of a style guide or template.

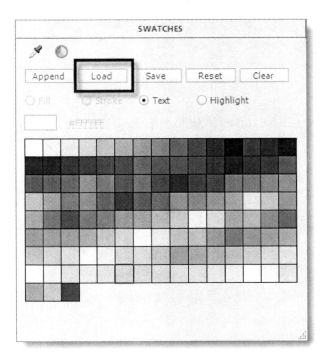

Using Themes

The fastest way to add visual design to your captivate projects in the absence of your own template is to use the preloaded Themes in Captivate. Captivate themes are pre-built templates. They blend backgrounds, styles, fonts, and layouts and give a quick consistent design to your project just by selecting one.

Enhanced Themes with New Theme Colors

In Captivate 8, each of the 11 themes now has a set over 20 preset groups of colors. You can further customize these colors allowing for many variations in the theme colors. You can also import color swatches from Adobe Photoshop.

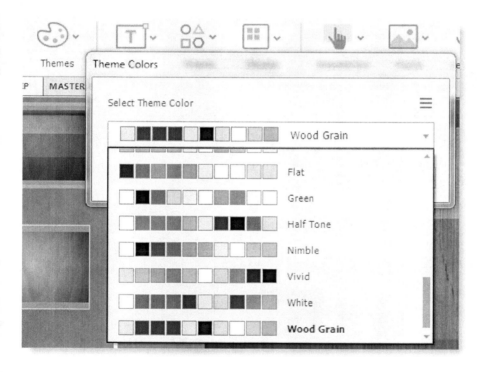

Loading and Editing Themes

To load and edit a theme:

1. Load one of the preset themes by clicking one on the Themes drop-down button.

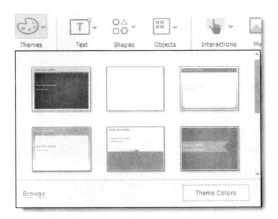

2. After loading a theme of your choice, you can further customize its colors at any time by clicking **Themes** > **Theme Colors**.

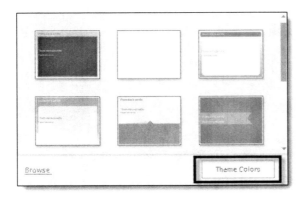

3. Choose from the huge combination of colors that are arranged in 20 preset groups.

4. You can even customize the colors in each set by clicking the **Customize** button on the **Theme Colors** window.

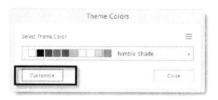

5. For each set, you can customize the colors of: **Title, Sub-title, Text 1, Text 2, Fill, Stroke, Slide Background, Skin 1, Skin 2, Skin 3**.

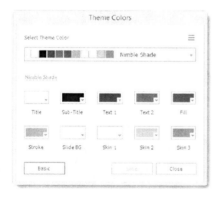

6. For the utmost control in the visual design of your project, use the **Slide Master** approach. Ensure that the Master Slide panel is open (**Window > Master Slide**). Add, delete and edit objects on the Master Slides to your desired specifications.

NOTE:

A quick approach to the visual design of your project is to load a Theme that is closest to what you want, then customize its colors in the Theme Colors window. Finally, you can tweak its appearance on the master slides.

7. Save your design as a new theme. **Themes > Save Theme As.**

Save your theme in a location and name that you can easily access. Captivate 8 saves the theme with a **.cptm** file extension.

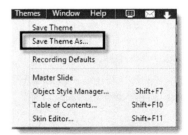

8. Load new themes you have created by clicking: **Themes** > **Browse** and navigate to where your theme is saved.

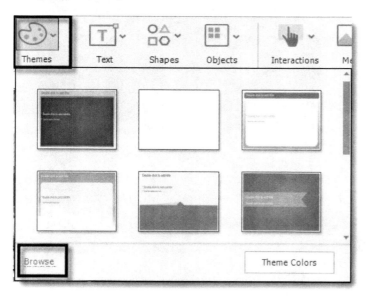

Creating Art and 3D Graphics for eLearning – The Piano Project

With its somewhat limited capabilities, you can still achieve a measure of artistic designs and 3d graphics right inside Captivate. The digital piano below is a Reusable Learning Object designed from inside Captivate 8 using a combination of

- Oval shapes
- Rectangular shapes
- Gradients
- Bevels
- Shadows

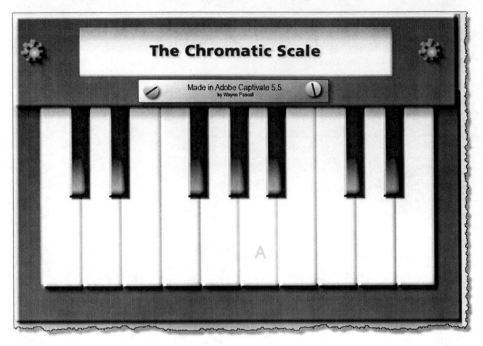

No external graphics were imported. It was created strictly using tools in Captivate 8. This means you can achieve the advantages of vector graphics by artistic uses of the tools inside Captivate 8. We will take a closer look how this interface was built and later on in this book we will add some functionality to the piano so that it actually plays musical notes.

What You Will Learn In This Tutorial

1. How to use **oval shapes** and **circles** to build parts of an interface

2. How to use different **line types** to build parts of an interface

2. How to use **rectangular shapes** to build parts of an interface

3. How to use **gradients** to achieve a 3D appearance and photo realism

4. How to use **bevel filters** to achieve a 3D appearance and photo realism

5. How to use **shadow effects** to achieve a 3D appearance and photo realism

Creating the Black Notes

1. In a Captivate project with dimensions 800x600 pixels, create the black piano key by first **clicking** the **Shapes** drop-down button

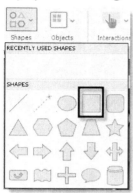

2. Click on the **Square** tool and create a rectangle with the following properties:

Stroke = Black

Width =2

Dimensions = (W32) x (H233)

The fill could be white for now, we will edit that next.

Eventually we want our rectangle to look like the image on the right.

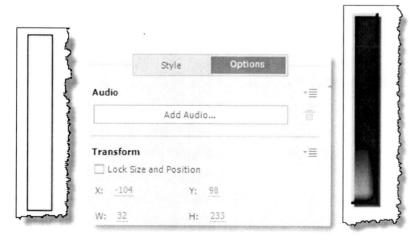

3. Click the rectangle to select it, and then click the **Fill** tool and the color palette window launches.

4. Click the first **Fill** tool and select **Gradient Fill**.

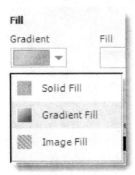

5. Click the second **Fill** tool and choose a **color** from the **top row** of colors that most closely matches the black gradient we are about to create.

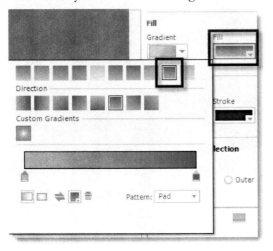

6. Choose a **Direction** from the **second row** that most closely matches the style of gradient you want to create. You can adjust this style later. This is a black linear gradient which is darker at top.

Next, we will add a shadow.

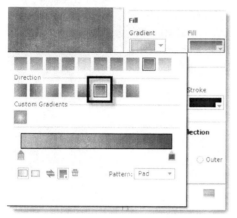

7. **Click** the **Color Stop** on the extreme **left** and choose a gray color. Click the **Color Stop** on the extreme **right** and choose a black color. Your image should look like the rectangle below. Right click it and edit the gradient to your liking as taught earlier in this chapter.

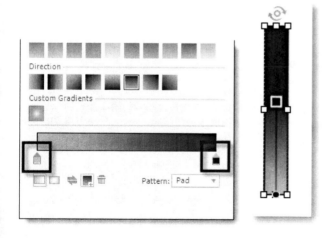

8. Before we create the shadow for our black key, it is important that we understand the interrelationship between **light** and **shadow** when creating art and three-dimensional objects. It is always good to imagine the **light** coming from a specific direction. The **shadow** will be cast in the opposite direction, behind the object. The **highlights and reflections** are usually on the same side of the light. Reflections are especially important if the material of the object is metallic, plastic or of a shiny nature. This is a key principle in creating realistic looking drawings, paintings and three-dimensional illustrations for eLearning projects.

We must be consistent in applying drop shadows on objects on a stage. If the shadow is cast in a North East direction for one object, it should be so for all objects on that stage, since this implies that the light coming from a South West direction.

In Captivate 8 we can create shadows using the **Shadow effect** and the highlights and three dimensional look using the **Bevel filter**. **Gradients** also give the illusion of light coming from a certain direction and adding realism to the object.

9. Click the rectangle to select it, and then open the **Shadow and Reflection** section in the Property Inspector and select a **preset** for a quick shadow type.

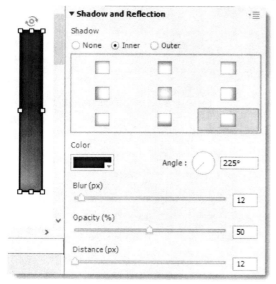

10.

The drop shadow in this project was created with the following properties:

- **Direction** –Inner
- **Angle** –225 degrees
- **Color** –Black (98%)
- **Blur** –12 px
- **Distance** –12px

11. To add a **bevel**, click the rectangle to select it, and then open the **Effects** tab (**Window > Effects**) and click **Add Effect > Filters > Bevel**

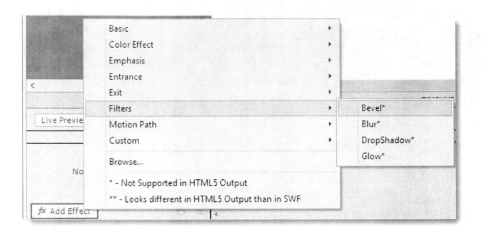

12. Create a bevel with the following properties:

- **Blur X** –2 px
- **Blur Y** –2 px
- **Strength** –80%

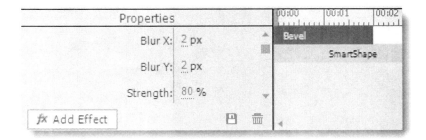

13. The resulting black note. We can now duplicate the black note as many
times as needed. Select all components of the note by clicking the mouse outside the
and dragging till all elements of the note are selected then hit Ctrl + D. Lock all
layers in the timeline to keep everything secure.

Later when we create the white notes, we'll bring all the black notes in front of the
white notes.

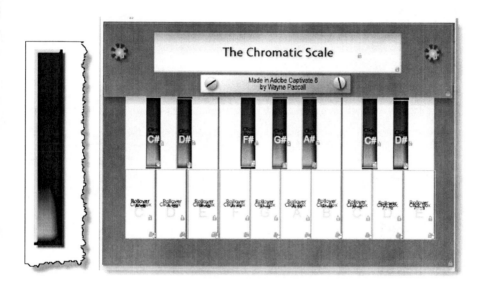

Creating the White Keys

14. We use the same techniques and tools described above to design the white
keys:

- **Rectangle**
- **White gradient**
- **Drop shadow**
- **Bevel**

Pencil and pen tools are still needed in Captivate, which will make this kind design and art much cleaner.

15. These notes were drawn and created in Flash. As you can see, they are more crisp and clearly defined because Flash has better drawing tools than Captivate.

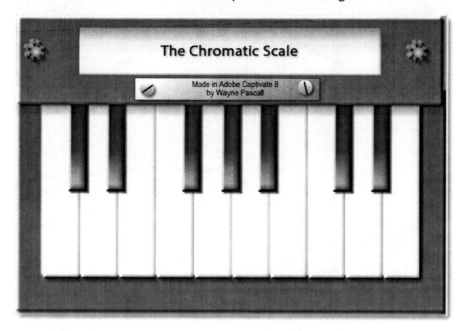

Arrange the notes so that the black ones are layered on top of the white ones and to resemble the picture above. Create the background using 2 rectangles. Add bevels and drop shadows to the rectangles that represent the body of the keyboard.

Lots can be done with Captivate 8 besides screen captures. Not only is it a powerful tool for designing and enhancing your own graphics and interfaces but you can also create sophisticated eLearning widgets and reusable learning objects. I created the one above as an eLearning tool to assist in understanding music theory, in particular, the chromatic scale. To learn how to use tools in Captivate that add functionality to the piano and make it an instructional tool, see chapter three, "Using Sound."

The next image is an iPod created solely in Captivate 8 using:

- **Shadows** (Inner)
- **Rectangles**
- **Gradients**
- **Circles with bevels**
- **Arrow heads**
- **Oval with gradient**

47

NOTE: You can use the principles taught here to create 3D graphics in Adobe Photoshop, Illustrator and even Flash. In these software, you can achieve more polished looking graphics and then import them into Captivate as vector graphics. Captivate recognizes and imports Photoshop .psd files.

The digital piano in the next page was designed entirely inside Flash using several layers of objects with gradients, bevels and shadows.

RESOURCES

Working Sample: www.elearnvisual.com/advanced-interactions.html

Captivate source files: www.elearnvisual.com/members.html

(Enter the above URL in your Web browser.)

Smart Shapes and Characters

In this chapter, we will be looking at how to use free-form smart shapes in a creative way to design master slides and in combination with characters to present a story.

What You Will Learn In This Tutorial

1. How to convert Smart Shapes to Free-form Objects

2. How to Edit Smart Shapes

3. How to use Smart Shapes to design Master Slides

4. How to Rotate Objects

5. How to use Characters to create story telling scenarios

6. How to use Smart Shapes with Characters

7. How to use PowerPoint to enhance Smart Shapes

8. How to create a perspective shadow in Captivate projects.

Using Free-form Smart Shapes

Smart Shapes in Captivate 8 is a nice new feature that presents opportunities for much creative work in projects. In this tutorial we will convert a Smart Shape into a Free-form object for designing a master slide.

1. First activate the master slide view by clicking: **Window > Master Slide**

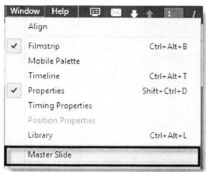

2. Add a **Rectangle shape** to a **blank Master Slide**.

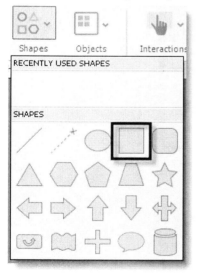

3. Position the **Smart Shape** at the top of the Master Slide as shown. Fill it with a color of your choice.

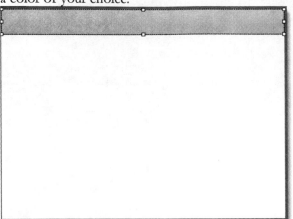

4. With the rectangle selected **right-click** and choose **Convert to Freeform**.

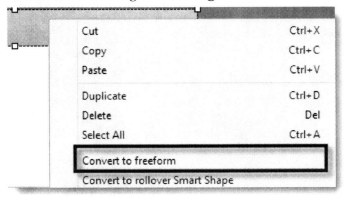

5. Four black points should appear on the corners of the rectangle if it is still selected. If the now Free-form Smart Object is unselected, **right-click** it and choose **Edit Points**.

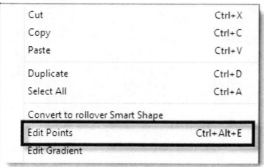

6. **Move your mouse** over one of the **four black points** at the corners of the rectangle till the mouse changes into a **double-arrow** then **click** the **black point**. Some **red editable points** should appear. In this example, we click the bottom-left black point.

7. **Click** one of the **red editable points** and drag to change the shape of the rectangle. In this example, we **drag downwards**.

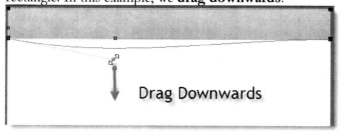

8. The rectangle acquires the new shape. Click the red point on the green handle and drag in desired direction to re-shape.

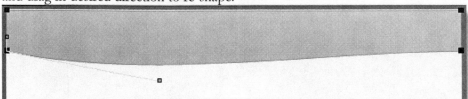

9. **Right-click** the new shape and click **Duplicate**.

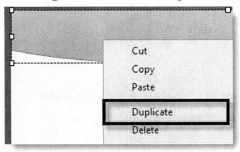

10. **Drag** the duplicate **free-form Smart Shape** to the bottom of the **Master Slide.**

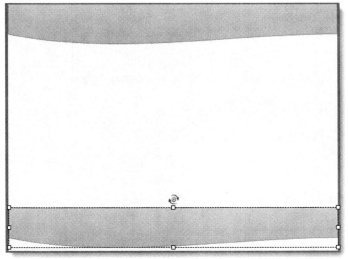

11. **Rotating** objects using the above method can be tricky and sometimes a little difficult to rotate the object in the exact desired angle. A more precise method is to use **the rotation tools** located in the **Transform** section of the Properties Inspector. There is a tool for **Rotate left**, **Rotate right** and entering the exact **Angle** of the rotation. For our example we, entered **180**

12. The Master Slide designed with Smart Shapes converted to free-form objects. You can use the technique taught here to convert Smart Shapes into varied artistic designs. If you fine-tune this technique combined with the use of gradients, bevels, reflections and shadows you can design lots of high quality vector graphics right inside Captivate 8.

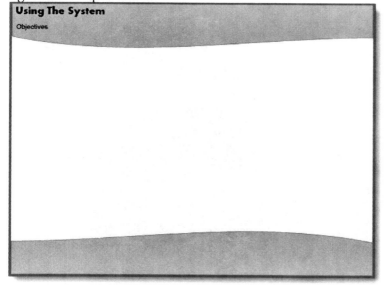

Saving Free-form Smart Shapes (New)

This new feature in Captivate 8, allows you save and reload freeform Smart Shapes you have created. To save a freeform Smart Shape:

1. Click the Smart Shape to select it.

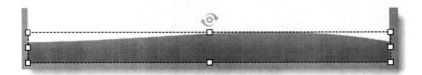

2. In the Properties panel, select **Save Shape** under the **Custom** section.

NOTE: The Custom section is activated **only** when you create a freeform Smart Shape.

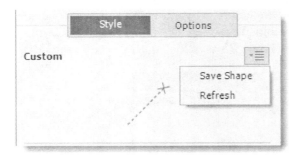

3. Name your new Smart Shape and click **OK**.

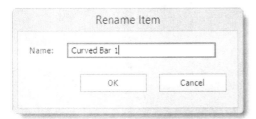

4. Your new Smart Shape appears in the list of available Smart Shapes.

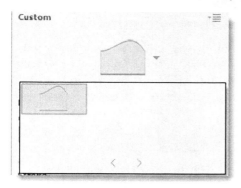

Using Characters for a Storytelling Scenario

Sometimes storytelling scenarios are used in eLearning to introduce training on a product, system or to add a personal touch to the training. This can be accomplished easily with the new features of **Characters** and **Smart Shapes** in Captivate 8. In this example we will use a combination of Characters and Smart Shapes with audio to tell a story.

New Characters and Poses

Captivate 8 now has new out-of-the-box assets, including 20 new characters, 50 different poses. This provides more options and flexibility than version 7 for using characters to tell a story or for scenario-based learning.

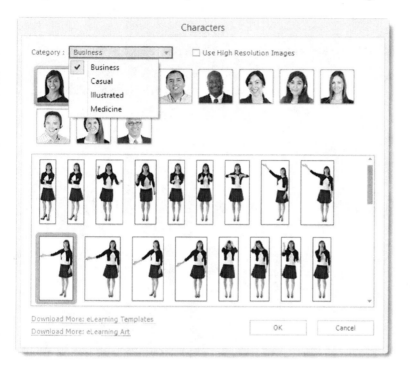

1. First, plan your story. Who are your characters? How many? What is the main message you want them to convey? The answer to these questions should help you create the dialogue between the characters. A simple storyboard in PowerPoint or right inside Captivate should be sufficient at this stage.

2. In Captivate 8, add as many characters as is needed to tell your story by clicking **Media > Characters**. Then choose from the available categories of: **Business, Casual, Illustrated** and **Medicine**, and choose from the available **poses.**

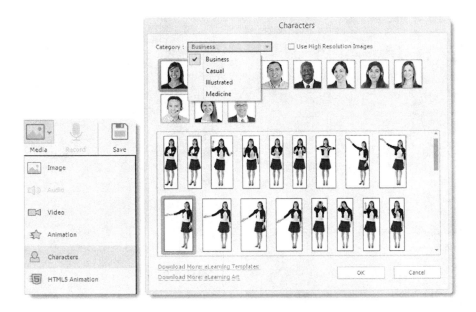

3. To create a sense of realism, let us add a shadow for each character. The shadow for each character on the right is a special kind of shadow called a **sun shadow** or **perspective shadow**. Captivate 8 will not allow you to create this kind of shadow. Captivate 8 creates just mere **drop shadows**. We will use **PowerPoint** to create this kind of shadow.

4. Copy /paste your character from Captivate to PowerPoint. Click the character in Captivate and press Ctrl + C (Copy) on the keyboard then click in an empty slide in PowerPoint and press Ctrl +V (Paste). Your character should have pasted into PowerPoint. Make the initial size of the character in Captivate as large as possible to fill almost the whole screen.

5. Click the character on the PowerPoint slide.

6. Click the Format tab in PowerPoint.

7. Click the **Picture Effects** tab.

8. Click **Shadow**.

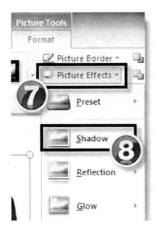

9. From the different Shadow options select a **Perspective** shadow (located at the bottom of all the preset shadows).

10. The character adopts the perspective shadow.

Now you can copy/

11. **Repeat** the above procedure for all characters in your story until all characters have a **perspective shadow**.

12. Now it' time to add some dialog between the characters. Let' add a **Callout** Smart Shape.

13. Insert a Callout Smart Shape by first clicking the Smart Shape tool and then select the **Rounded Callout.** Drag your mouse over an empty area on the stage.

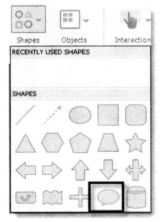

14. **Position** the **Callout** and **pointer** over each character to represent speech. **Right-click** the Callout Smart Shape and choose **Add Text** to add text to your character's speech bubble. Repeat this for each character in your story.

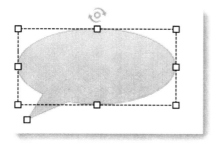

15. For each slide, **add characters and text** till your story is complete.

16. If you will add **audio** for each character, they should be **synchronized in the timeline**. For example, in the conversation above, the audio for Janet should appear earlier in the timeline than the audio for Ed.

RESOURCES
Captivate source files: www.elearnvisual.com/members.html
(Enter the above URL in your Web browser).

3 – GETTING CREATIVE WITH ANIMATIONS

User Triggered Captivate Animations

One of the most under-used actions in Captivate is the "**Apply Effect**" action. So instead of the traditional "Go to Next Slide" and "Go to Previous Slide" actions, we can have an effect or animation that is triggered when the user clicks somewhere. This has many creative opportunities for creating movement and interest in an otherwise dull course.

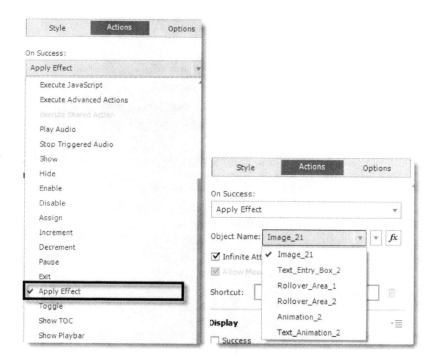

Example: you can have a pile of images over each other on the screen. One slides over to the right and disappears each time a button is clicked, revealing the next image below. The application of this effect is limited only by imagination.

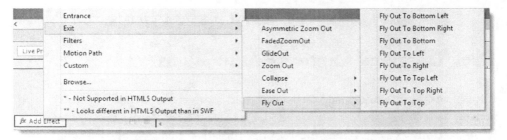

In the example below, we will use a user triggered animation to create a Zoom in / Zoom out effect on an image.

Zoom In / Zoom Out Effect

In previous sections, we looked at the creative uses of filters and effects to create visually appealing graphics in Captivate. Now we are going to look at a creative use of one these filters and effects to add interactive objects to eLearning projects. We will create a Zoom in /Zoom out effect for an image or group of images.

1. Add an **image** to the stage to which you want to apply the Zoom in/Zoom out effect. Please note that this is not the Zoom Area from Captivate' Standard Objects. We will be using some animation effects that will be activated when a **Click Box** is clicked. Note the **Item Name** of the image. You will need this later to program the actions. You can also change the Item Name to one of your choice.

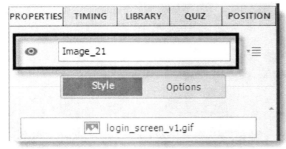

2. Add a graphic with (+) and (-) signs, over which you will add your zoom click boxes. Alternatively, you can use two Text Buttons. One for zoom in, the other for zoom out.

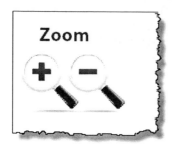

3. Add two Click Boxes, one each over the (+) and (-) signs, the other for zoom out. **Click** the Click Box over the **(+)** sign. We will program a zoom in effect for the graphic here.

4. Under the **Action** tab, click the **On Success** drop-down menu and select **Apply Effect**.

5. In the **Object Name** drop-down menu select the item on which you want to apply the effect. In this case, it is our **Image_21**.

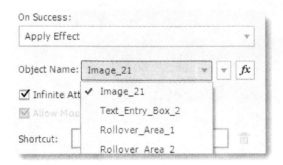

6. Click the **Animation Palette button**. It is critical that you perform this step. It links the image to the animation effect you are about to create.

7. Under the **Effects** tab, click **Add Effect** > **Basic** > **ScaleTo**

8. Select the amount of **Scale** on the X and Y axes. We have set it at 1.3. Double-click to change. This means every time we click the Click Box, it will increase the size of Image_44 by a factor of 1.3.

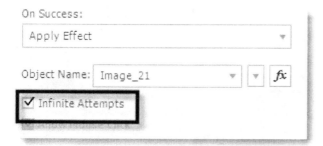

9. With the Click Box selected, under the Action tab, ensure that the option for **Infinite attempts** is selected.

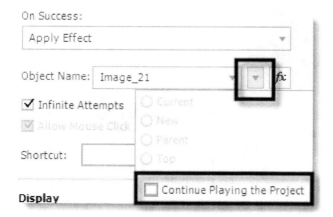

10. With the Click Box selected, under the Action tab, click the second drop-down menu next to Object Name and ensure that **Continue Playing the Project** is NOT checked.

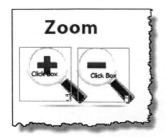

11. To create the Zoom out effect, repeat the above steps for the Click Box over the (-) sign. In this case we will reverse the effect of the scale. Select the amount of **Scale** on the X and Y axes. Double-click and set it to 0.9 or anything less than 1.0. This means every time we click the Click Box, it will increase the size of Image_44 by a factor of 0.9.

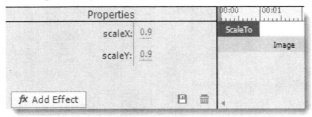

Clicking the **(+)** and **(-)** signs will zoom the picture in and out as many times as you click. This feature can be useful for users who are visually impaired, to examine an object on the screen more closely, to zoom into a grid with data among other uses.

RESOURCES

Captivate source files: www.elearnvisual.com/members.html

(Enter the above URL in your Web browser).

Using HTML5 Animations

The Importance of HTML5

HTML (*HyperText Markup Language*) 5 is the 5th revision and the latest version of HTML. It is the coding language that developers use to build web pages and applications, allowing internet users to enjoy the modern multimedia features of the web and mobile devices without having to resort to proprietary plug-ins. HTML5 therefore makes it possible for designers and developers to build applications that are accessible from any browser, any desktop, and any mobile device, anywhere at any time. It offers greater possibilities for asynchronous learning and cloud computing. Web pages and applications coded in HTML5 can be accessed by desktop and mobile users.

With the advent of the iPhone, iPad and Android devices, new possibilities for eLearning were born. Now users can log into an LMS and access courses from their mobile phones. This new field of mLearning (mobile learning) is growing rapidly as there continues to be a slew of releases in android tablets to compete with the renowned iPad.

HTML5 is the solution for mobile devices such as the iPad that do not support the Flash plug-in. Since a significant amount of eLearning like the ones developed in Captivate, are published in Flash format, it is essential to publish eLearning in HTML5 format for users with mobile devices that do not support Flash. HTML5 technology is still in development and will continue to evolve and be refined as the Web 2.0 era marches on.

mLearning is here to stay and will continue to grow with the mobile industry. Adobe announced in November 9, 2011 that it is abandoning its development of Flash for mobile devices and instead is focusing on mobile development of HTML5 for mobile devices. Captivate 8 is now loaded with the ability to publish projects in HTML5 format and specifically for the iPad and iPhone using Responsive projects. You can now import HTML5 and Edge Animations directly into Adobe Captivate. Position and resize the animations where you like and publish to HTML5 format. This presents lots of opportunities for enhanced interactivity beyond what can be created inside Captivate.

HTML5 Animations in Responsive Projects

HTML5 animations open the door for lots of creativity in Captivate projects because you can add some flair beyond the capabilities of Captivate. You can develop your animations in an external program like Adobe Flash or Edge Animate and then import them into Captivate. There are some online tools where you can quickly create HTML5 animations in the form of games and educational interactions. For example, **Elearning Brothers** has an online tool called **Interaction Builder** that does this very thing well and quickly using templates that you can customize. You end up with a polished, interactive widget or game that you have created in as short a time as 5 minutes. It is as easy as adding text, images, audio if any, customizing colors and publishing to Flash or HTML5.

If you are adding HTML5 animations for the purpose of publishing for **mobile devices**, you should first load a **Responsive project** template. Publishing for users of mobile devices through Responsive projects, specifically the iPad, is a great new feature in Captivate 8. In Responsive projects, Captivate creates different layouts called Breakpoints for primary, tablet and mobile (phone) devices. You can even override the placement and size of objects in each breakpoint with your own adjustments.

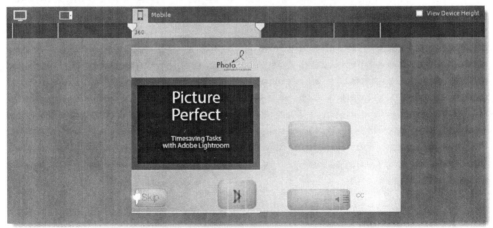

To publish Captivate projects so that they run correctly on mobile devices, you need to first load the **Responsive Project** template.

1. Click: **File > New > Responsive Project** OR Click **New** on the Welcome screen.

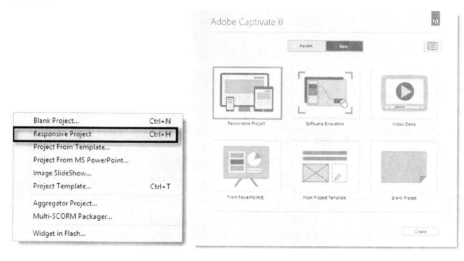

2. On the welcome screen click Responsive Project

3. Click **Create**

4. To publish your Responsive project, click File > Publish.

5. Choose your publish options. Gesture Configuration and Geolocation are new features that enhance usability for mobile devices. **Geolocation** uses GPS technology to determine the location of users of your course. You can then use this information to customize the course material based on their location. There are creative possibilities here to customize a course based on people's location.

Importing HTML5 Animations

You can insert HTML5 animations built by Adobe Edge Animate or other software in two formats: **.oam**, or **.zip**.

To insert an HTML5 animation into your project:

1. Click: **Media > HTML5 Animation.**

2. Navigate to the location of your HTML5 animation.

3. Click Open.

4. Place the animation in the desired location

5. Run the **HTML5 Tracker** for any possible issues.

While developing, run the **HTML5 Tracker** (Project > HTML5 Tracker) occasionally to verify what is supported in HTML5 format and if there are any errors. Not all objects and interactions are supported on the iPad. You cannot use Drag and Drop interactions in responsive projects and this feature is disabled in Captivate when in the responsive project mode.

It is a great idea while working on responsive projects to keep the **HTML5 Tracker** open at all times, so you can constantly monitor what objects and interactions are not supported in HTML 5 output. Click **Window > HTML5 Tracker** to have it opened as a tab.

4 – GETTING CREATIVE WITH AUDIO AND TEXT-TO-SPEECH

Using Rollover Slidelets

Rollover Slidelets are powerful interactive elements that allow users of your content to access **images, text, audio and video** through one mouse rollover. The creative possibilities are as many as your imagination allows.

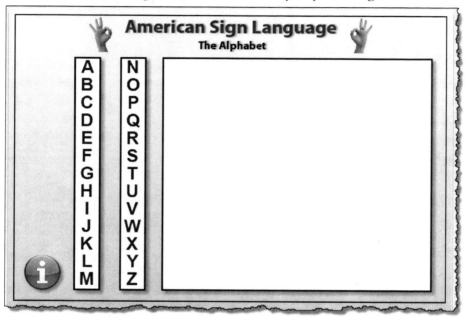

In this chapter we will create a reusable learning object to teach the alphabet of American Sign Language. We will use Rollover Slidelets to display both the hand signal and the corresponding letter of the alphabet.

What You Will Learn In This Tutorial

1. How to **add** a **Rollover Slidelet**

2. How to **configure** a **Rollover Slidelet** to display image and text

3. How to use **Rollover Slidelets** in **creative ways**

The American Sign Language Project

1. Prepare two sections of the screen for content, one for the **letters of the alphabet**, the other for the **Rollover Slidelets**. In this example, we have used three rectangles.

2. Add a "**More Information Icon**" We hold place a Rollover Slide here loaded with brief information text and audio about American Sign Language.

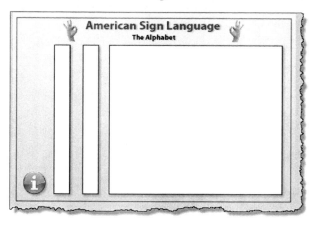

3. Add the letters of the Alphabet in two columns on the left.

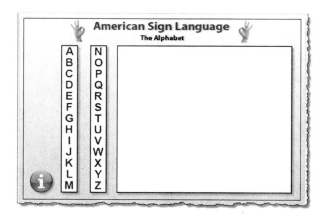

4. Add a Rollover Slidelet over the letter **A**.

To insert a **Rollover Slidelet**, click **Objects > Rollover Slidelet.**

5. Choose the **border color**, **border**, **transparency**, **transition effect** and other attributes of the **Rollover Slidelet** (the "hot spot" that triggers the Slidelet when the mouse rolls over it). In this example, we have:

- De-selected **Show border**

- Selected **Show Runtime Border**

6. Position the **Rollover Slidelet** (the "hot spot" that triggers the Slidelet when the mouse rolls over it) over the letter **A,** and the **Slidelet** over the rectangular space.

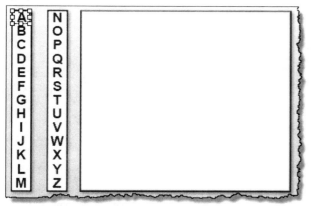

7. Click the **Slidelet** and insert an image of the hand signal for the letter **A.** With the Slidelet selected, you can also insert a caption entitled **A.**

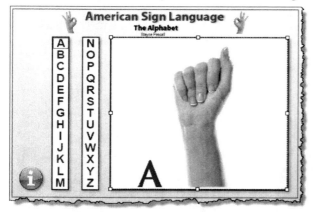

8. Configure the **settings** on the **Slidelet** and its contents. In this example, the contents of the Slidelet (Image of the hand) has a **timing** of 7 seconds and **transition** is set to **fade in and out**. The Slidelet is set to **display for rest of Slide**.

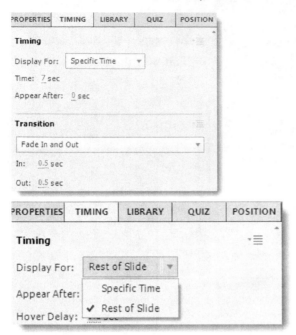

9. The Rollover Slidelet for the letter A at runtime.

Repeat the above steps for the other 25 letters of the Sign Language alphabet.

Tip: **Lock** all previous Slidelets before adding an additional one. Once you have gotten the first Rollover Slidelet working properly, simply duplicate it, and then lock it. Now you can edit the duplicate to create a new Slidelet without messing up your previous work.

Note:

*The Slidelet has its own **timeline**. You can adjust the timing of the Slidelet's objects (Image, text, video and audio) inside its timeline. Simply click on a Slidelet to access its timeline. Remember the Slidelet is the section that contains the image, text, audio or video.*

RESOURCES
Working Sample: www.elearnvisual.com/advanced-interactions.html
Captivate source file: www.elearnvisual.com/members.html
(Enter the above URL in your Web browser.)

The Piano Project

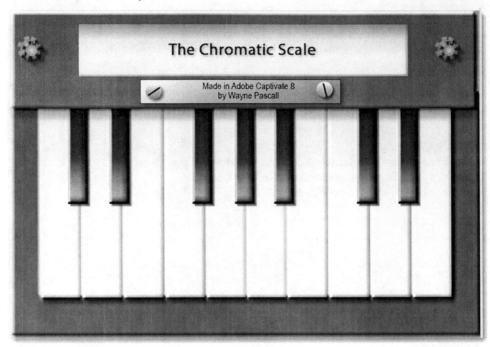

In a previous chapter we created a digital piano using the drawing tools of Captivate, then created a three dimensional look using a combination gradients, shadows and bevels.

In this chapter we are going to add some functionality to the piano using sound. An important feature in Captivate 8 for creative audio projects is the "**Play Audio**" action. We will accomplish the playing audio action by using a click box over each note that activates a sound file. We will also add a Rollover Caption over each note to identify it with a key in the chromatic Scale.

1.
Before we begin adding sound to the piano, ensure that all parts on the timeline are **locked**. Lock all elements by clicking the lock sign at the top next to the eye icon. This will ensure that none of our previous work will get accidentally moved out of place as we begin adding Rollover Captions and Click Boxes.

Rollover_Area_48		Rollover A...
Rollover_Area_47		Rollover A...
Rollover_Area_46		Rollover A...
Rollover_Area_45		Rollover A...
Click_Box_100		Click Box:...
Click_Box_99		Click Box:...

0.0s

Tip:
Add an invisible button that pauses the timeline at 1.5 seconds.

2.
Add a **Click Box** to each of the 17 keys on the piano, **linking** each Click Box to a corresponding **sound file**.

Click Box 1 –Note 1 –C

Click Box 2 –Note 2 –C#

Click Box 3 –Note 3 –D

Click Box 4 –Note 4 –D#

Click Box 5 –Note 5 –E

Click Box 6 –Note 6 –F

Click Box 7 –Note 7 –F#

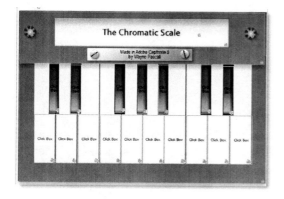

3. Click the **first Click Box** on the left of the piano over the first white note of the piano. This is the note of **C**. In the **Action** section of the Properties Inspector, select **Play Audio** as the **On Success** action.

4. Click the **folder icon** and navigate to where the **sound file** (Piano tone for the note C) is located and select it.

Ensure that the checkbox for **Infinite** attempts is checked.

5. **Repeat** the above procedure for **all Click Boxes** on the piano, until all keys with Click Boxes are assigned a sound. A C piano tone to the **first white note**, then a **C#** (C Sharp) on **second Click Box (First Black Note)** and so on. There are many sites on the Internet such as sounddogs.com, from where you can purchase the piano tones.

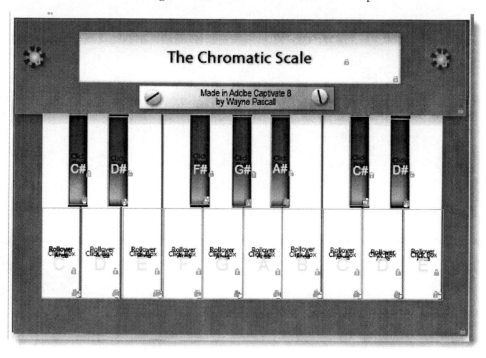

Text-to-Speech

Pros in Using Text-to-Speech

- Cheap means of adding voice over media
- Do not have or cannot afford the cost of recording equipment, facilities and voice over talent
- Very low costs for retakes of audio after quality reviews
- Able to perform instant edits of the audio at any time
- Fast turnaround times in adding audio for narrations
- An added media in the project to aid users with visual and physical disabilities.
-

Cons in Using Text-to-Speech

- Depending on the installed "voices" some expressions may have a robotic sound
- May need to use extra punctuation and VTML tags to assist in the pronunciation of certain words

New Text-to-Speech Voices

In addition to "Paul" and "Kate", Captivate 8 is loaded with 4 additional text-to-speech voices. Here is the total list:

- **Kate**: English female voice
- **Paul**: English male voice
- **Bridget**: British English female voice
- **James**: British English female voice
- **Julie**: US English female voice
- **Chloe**: Canadian French female voice
- **Yumi**: Korean voice

Suggested Voices for Text-to-Speech

"Voices" are the files that provide the information for conversion of the text to audio. They must be installed on your computer for the conversion to occur. The text-to-speech feature is upgraded in Captivate 8 more Loquendo voices. Captivate 8 will also load all voices installed in your system in addition to the ones shipped with the software. Here are some realistic sounding voices that you can purchase:

- **IVONA** - Eric, Jennifer, Kendra, Joey, Kimberly, Salli (Teenage), Ivy (Child), Brian (UK), Emma (UK)

  (#1 Recommendation)

- **Neospeech** voices included in Captivate 8.

- **AT&T Natural Voices** - Mike, Rich, Crystal, Alberto and Rosa (Spanish)

- **Acapela Group** - Aaron, Heather, Laura, Ryan, Graham (UK), Lucy (UK)

- **Cepstral** - Allison, David, Diane, William, Lawrence (UK), Millie (UK)

Improving the Quality of Text-to-Speech

1. Audio Bitrates

Encode all audio mp3 files in the project at a bitrate of no less than 128 kilobits per second (kbps).

Click **Audio > Settings** and choose **CD Bitrate (128 kbps)**.

Although this will increase the file size somewhat, it's better to have clean sounding audio at the expense of a slight increase in file size than to have a small file hosting poor quality audio. Audio mp3 files encoded at 128 kbps is near CD quality and is the lowest standard used for online music stores such as iTunes and Rhapsody.

2. Use High Quality SAPI5 Voices Encoded at 16 KHz

The **Speech Application Programming Interface (SAPI)** is an API developed by Microsoft to allow the use of speech recognition and speech synthesis within Windows applications. Earlier text-to-speech technology used SAPI1 through 4 voices such as Microsoft Mary, Mike and Sam. These had a very robotic sound. With the introduction of SAPI5, the quality of the voices has improved significantly. SAPI5 voices were first released in 2000. Ensure that you are using SAPI5 voices. The ones listed below are excellent choices.

The IVONA voices are amazingly clean and of a high quality. Remember that audio encoded at 16 KHz is of a higher quality than audio at 8 kHz. For professional purposes, ensure that you are using the 16 kHz voices. Telephone speech is usually encoded at 64Kbs at a sampling rate of 8 KHz. 16 KHz voices are recommended for eLearning material that will be hosted on a web server, LMS or Disc.

3. Punctuation

Use punctuation such as commas, exclamation marks, question marks and periods in convenient places to aid in readability and tone of the narration. Commas are especially important in text-to-speech work. You may need to add extra commas that were not in the original script to improve the flow of the narration.

4. VTML Tags

Use VTML (Voice Text Markup Language) tags to achieve powerful control of pitch, speed, volume, pauses and pronunciation of specific sections and words of the narration.

Using this powerful hidden gem in text-to-speech projects helps you control the generated speech and improve its tonal quality.

Parameters

Pitch

This value defines the pitch of the synthesized voice. A pitch with a value of 100(%) is normal. The possible pitch range is 50- 200(%). The higher the pitch value, the higher the pitch.

Speed

This value defines the speed of the synthesized voice. A speed with a value of 100(%) is normal. The possible speed range is 50 - 400%. The higher the speed value, the higher the speed.

Volume

This value defines the speed of the synthesized voice. A speed with a value of 100(%) is normal. The possible speed range is 0 - 500%. The higher the volume value, the louder the volume.

Pause

This value defines the length of pause of the synthesized voice. A pause with a value of 687(msec) is normal. The range is 0 - 65535(msec). The higher the pause value, the longer the pause.

Useful VTML tags

PAUSE

Your**<vtml_pause time="msec"/>**Text

Replace the **msec** with amount of milliseconds to pause.

Example:

Your**<vtml_pause time="80"/>**Text

To pause 80 milliseconds.

BREAK

Your**<vtml_break level="0,1 or 2"/>**Text

0 = Continuous

1= Minor break

2= Major break

Example:

Your**<vtml_break level="1"/>**Text

To create a minor break in reading. Duration is shorter than a pause tag.

PITCH

<vtml_pitch value="pitch">Your Text**</vtml_pitch>**

Where **pitch** can be 1-200. 100 is normal pitch

Example:

<vtml_pitch value="120">Your Text**</vtml_pitch>**

To increase the pitch slightly.

SPEED

<vtml_speed value="speed">Your Text**</vtml_speed>**

Where **speed** can be 1-200. 100 is normal pitch

Example:

<vtml_speed value="80">Your Text**</vtml_speed>**

To decrease the speed slightly.

PRONUNCIATION

<vtml_sub alias="string">Your Text**</vtml_sub>**

Where **string** is replaced with what will be spoken instead of the Word(s).

Example:

<vtml_sub alias="Jim">Gym**</vtml_sub>**

To pronounce "Gym" as "Jim."

VOLUME

<vtml_volume value="0-300">Your Text**</vtml_volume>**

Where **volume** can be 0 (silent) to 300 (loudest).

Example:

<vtml_volume value="150">Your Text**</vtml_volume>**

"Your Text" pronounced at a moderate volume.

Assignment: Using Paul from Neospeech

Try using the text-to-speech feature in Captivate 8 to convert the sentences below to audio. Try using with and without the provided VTML tags and compare the results. Experiment with different tags and voices.

1. Comparison One:

Without VTML tags

Don't, ever, lift a heavy item using your back.

Versus

With VTML tags
Don't, **<vtml_pitch value="120">**ever, **</vtml_pitch>**lift a heavy item using your back.

2. Comparison Two:

Without VTML tags

Hello, welcome to this exciting new course on computer ergonomics.

versus

With VTML tags

Hello, welcome to this**<vtml_pitch value="120">** exciting **</vtml_pitch>**new course**<vtml_speed value="90">**on computer **<vtml_break level="1"/><vtml_sub alias="er-gonomics">** ergonomics**</vtml_sub></vtml_speed>**.

If you listened carefully, both Paul and Kate (Two of the voices loaded with Captivate 8) had problems pronouncing "computer ergonomics." The problem is the "ter" syllable in "computer" sounds too similar to "er," the beginning syllable in "ergonomics." The installed voices struggle to differentiate between the two syllables making the resulting sound, very robotic. The solution is to add a **break tag** that creates a brief break in time between the two words and add an **alias tag** that helps the voices to pronounce "ergonomics" properly. Please note, in using VTML tags, there should be no spaces between the tags and words in normal format.

Text-to-Speech in the American Sign Language Project

Converting the Text to Audio

1. Load the American Sign Language Project from the previous chapter. There we added a Rollover Slidelet for the letter A. In this exercise, we are going to add audio that sounds the letter ""using Text-to-speech.

First, we will make Captivate convert the text to audio, and then we will import the audio from the library into the Slidelet.

2. Under the **Slide Notes** tab (Window > Slide Notes), click the (**+**) sign to add slide notes.

3. Enter the **text** you want converted to audio. In this case we will enter the letter A.

4. Place a **check mark** in the "**TTS**" box. .

5. Click on the "**Text-to-Speech**" conversion tool.

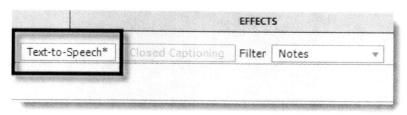

6. Choose one of the **TTS voices**: Kate, Paul or one of your installed voices, then click **Save** & **Generate Audio**.

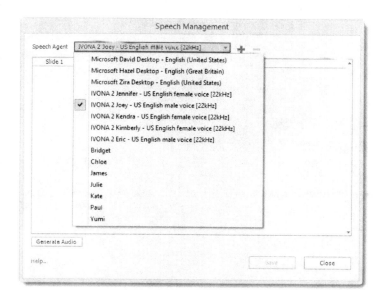

7. The text is converted to speech based on the voice chosen.

8. Captivate adds the audio file for your converted text to the main timeline of the slide.

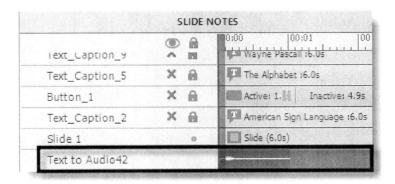

9. **Right-click** the audio file in the main timeline and choose **Find in the Library**.

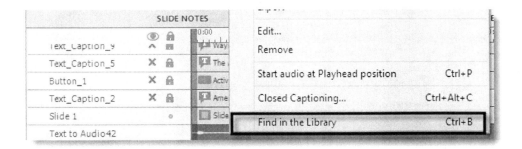

10. Captivate highlights the audio in the library. **Double-click** it.

◀)) Text to Aud... 44.82   1
◀)) Text to Aud... 49.86   1
◀)) Text to Aud... 91.98   0
◀)) Text to Aud... 91.98   1

11. The **Audio Properties** window launches. Give the audio file a **name** you can easily identify later. In this example, we have **renamed** it "**Text to Audio –A.**" Click **OK**.

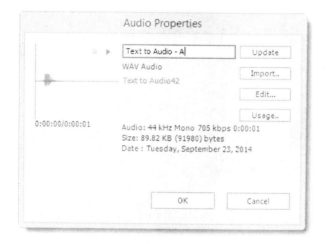

12. Remove the audio from the slide by **right-clicking** it in the timeline and selecting **Remove**.

What we have just done is use Captivate to convert the letter A to a speech file. Captivate by default, puts Text-to-speech converted files in the main timeline of the slide.

We need this file in the Rollover Slidelet instead of the main timeline. We will now place this audio file in the Slidelet.

				Edit...
Text_Caption_9	⊙ 🔒	0:00		Remove
Text_Caption_5	✕ 🔒			Start audio at Playhead position
Button_1	✕ 🔒			
Text_Caption_2	✕ 🔒			Closed Captioning...
Slide 1	⊙			Find in the Library
Text to Audio42				

Importing the Audio into the Slidelet

1. **Click** the **Slidelet** to select it.

2. Locate the audio file we converted earlier: **Text to Audio –A** in the library (Window > Library) and **drag** it unto the Slidelet.

▼ 🔊 Audio
     🔊 (Clip)AMERICAN SI...   4484.70 1
     🔊 Text to Audio11 - A   36.72   1
     🔊 Text to Audio12 - B   44.82   1
     🔊 Text to Audio13 - C   49.86   1
     🔊 Text to Audio41   91.98   0

3. The audio is added to the timeline of the Rollover Slidelet. Test the rollover Slidelet. You should see the hand signal for the letter A and simultaneously hear it's audio.

Repeat the above steps for adding audio for the other 25 letters of the alphabet.

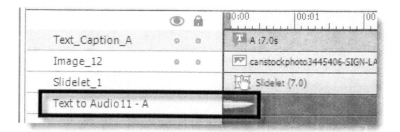

RESOURCES

Working Sample: www.elearnvisual.com/advanced-interactions.html
Captivate source file: www.elearnvisual.com/members.html

(Enter the above URL in your Web browser.)

5 – USING 508 COMPLIANCE

What Is 508 Compliance?

508 Compliance refers to a set of guidelines and standards for electronic and information technologies that enhance usability for people with disabilities. The law is aimed at assisting people with four types of impairments:

- Vision
- Hearing
- Speech
- Motion/Dexterity

The standards are governed by Section 508 of the **Rehabilitation Act of 1973** (29 U.S.C. 794d). Congress amended and strengthened 508 Compliance with the **Workforce Investment Act of 1998** to further enhance accessibility for people with disabilities.

The Impact of Section 508 Compliance

All federal government agencies are required to ensure that their electronic and information technologies are 508 compliant. Organizations and corporations in the private sector that have a key concern about making their digital information more accessible to people with disabilities have also implemented 508 Compliance into their systems. It requires meticulous work to ensure that these requirements are met. This means that websites, course materials on an LMS and all forms of eLearning and computer-based training should be accessible to people with disabilities.

Users who are visually impaired for example, may be relying on screen readers to assist them. They should be able to navigate through your content using the Tab key, or shortcut keys. They should also be provided with ALT texts for every multimedia element on a screen and closed captions for audio. When designing eLearning, consideration should also be given for people with hearing disabilities, color blindness, people with photosensitive epilepsy, people who may be physically disabled due to muscular dystrophy, stroke, carpal tunnel syndrome, partial paralysis or anything that disables normal movement of limbs.

Implementing 508 Compliance

Here are some guidelines for achieving 508 Compliance in your eLearning projects.

Color

- Avoid using colors that are used as the only method for identifying screen elements or controls.

- Avoid using the colors red and green if possible.

- The screen may become unusable for persons who are color blind, with low vision or fully blind.

- People who are color blind may not see the colors red and green.

Images, videos, animations, buttons

- All images, videos and animations and buttons should have **accessibility text** that describes each multimedia element. In Captivate, this should go beyond checking "Auto Label" which is usually not descriptive enough to help an impaired user. Manually enter some descriptive text. A "Next" image button should therefore be accompanied with the accessibility text "Next."

- Screen readers like JAWS will read aloud the accessibility text to aid visually impaired persons.

Audio

- All audio and narration should be accompanied with **closed captions** that are textual equivalents of spoken audio.

- For persons with hearing disabilities.

Navigation

- Disabled users should be able to navigate through different objects on the screen using the **Tab key** on a Qwerty keyboard.

- For persons with physical disabilities that make it difficult for them to use a mouse or type.

Slide Notes

- Supply **accessibility text** for individual slides that screen readers can read. This can be imported from the slide notes.

- Screen readers like JAWS will read aloud the accessibility text to aid visually impaired persons.

Flickering Objects

- Avoid using text, flash or animation objects that flicker, flash or blink at intensities of over 2 Hz or lower than 55 Hz.

- This can trigger an epileptic seizure in people suffering from photo-sensitive epilepsy.

Adding Accessibility Text

1. To add **accessibility text** to an object, first **select it** by clicking on it.

2. Select **Accessibility** from the drop-down button under the **Properties** tab.

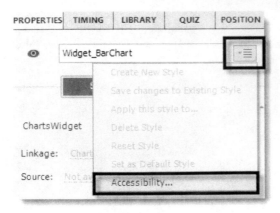

3. Enter a label and some descriptive text about the object.

4. Captivate 8 has additional features for establishing 508 compliance. You can also specify the **Tab Order** for interactive objects as well as directly import slide notes into the Accessibility panel. As mentioned earlier in this chapter, a disabled user can use the **Tab Key** to navigate through different objects on the screen. Establishing the Tab Order determines the order in which the object are navigated. This is especially helpful for screen reading software that aid the blind, visually disabled and physically disabled learners.

To establish the Tab Order, first click the **slide** on the filmstrip, then select **Tab Order** from the drop-down button under the **Properties** tab.

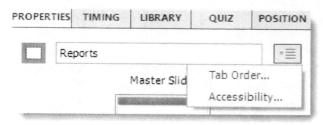

5. Use the **Up (↑) and Down (↓) arrows** to establish the order you would like a possible disabled learner to navigate through the interactive objects listed, then press **OK**.

6. A quick way to add accessibility text for objects is to use your slide notes. To import slide notes into the Accessibility panel, **click** the **Slide** on the filmstrip, then select **Accessibility** from the drop-down button under the **Properties** tab.

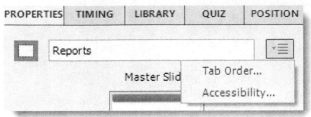

7. Click **Import Slide Notes** and the slide notes populate the **Slide Accessibility** panel.

Adding Closed Captions

Adding closed captions in your learning modules is significant for accommodating learners with hearing disabilities. If closed captions are configured in the content of your courses, a learner can simply turn them on by clicking the closed caption button in the Captivate interface. They will then be presented with the text equivalent of all narration in the lessons. Adding closed captions for all audio files of recorded speech is one of the requirements for achieving 508 Compliance.

1. To add closed captions to a slide; first ensure that the Slide Notes panel is open by clicking:

Window / Slide Notes.

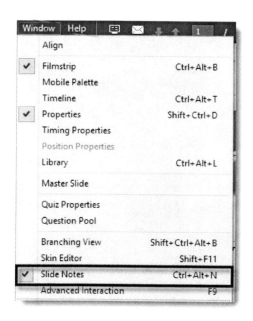

2. To add closed captions, simply type the notes in the **Slide Notes** panel and place a **check mark** under the **Audio CC** box in the **Slide Notes** panel.

For the first quarter of 2007, sales grew by 45%. In January, software accounted for 30% of the sales.

3. To edit the closed captions **font**, click the **Closed Captioning** button in the **Slide Notes** panel.

4. Click the **CC Project Settings** button in Closed Captioning window that launches.

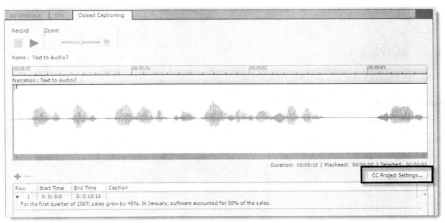

5. The **CC Project Settings** window launches. Choose your **Family** and **Size** of **Font**.

6. Synchronize the flow of the closed captions with the audio, using the **Closed Captioning** window. Click the Play button and while listening to the audio, add new lines of text to flow with the audio by clicking the plus (+) button. Each time you click the plus (+) button, a draggable marker is added in the audio display. These markers are numbered, signifying where the next line of text begins. Fine tune the synchronization by dragging them to the correct spots in the audio display.

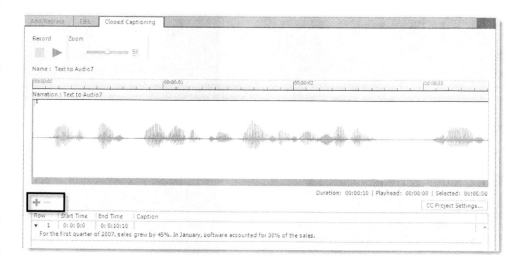

The American Sign Language Project

1. Open the **American Sign Language project** from the previous chapter where we added text-to-speech. We will now add 508 Compliance to this reusable learning object.

2. Click all captions, images and objects **outside** of the Rollover Slidelet and add **accessibility text** as described earlier in this chapter.

3. Click the Slidelet and add **accessibility text** for the hand signal and caption according to the guidelines described earlier in this chapter.

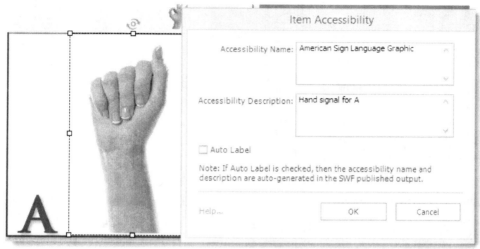

4. Unbelievable as it may seem, Captivate 8 still does **not** have a way to add **closed captions** for the **audio inside a Slidelet**. Closed captions can be added only to audio in the main timeline and not the timeline of the Slidelet . This should be an essential addition for future upgrades.

Note: Remember, part of 508 Compliance is that disabled users who may not be able to aptly use a mouse or type, should be able to navigate through different objects on the screen using the **Tab key** or **Shortcut Keys.** In this project, we will add a shortcut key for each letter of the sign language alphabet. Key A for A, key B for B, C for C and so on.

In this way, a disabled user can activate the entire Slidelet for the sign A simply by pressing the A key.

5. Click the **Rollover Slidelet** (hotspot).

6. In the **Properties** Inspector, under the **Actions** tab, click the **Shortcut** field.

7. On your computer' keyboard, **press** the **Key** that you would like use as a shortcut for activating this Rollover Slidelet. In this example, we have pressed the key **A**.

8. The Rollover Slidelet for the sign A is activated every time the user presses the key **A**.

Repeat the above steps for the other 25 letters in the American Sign Language project.

RESOURCES:

- Section508.gov Website – www.section508.gov

Working Sample: www.elearnvisual.com/advanced-interactions.html

Captivate source file: www.elearnvisual.com/members.html

(Enter the above URL in your Web browser.)

6 – USING FLASH

Creating New Widgets in Flash

File > New Project > Widget in flash

Editing Captivate Projects in Flash

1. Exporting the Captivate Project to Flash:
File > New Project > Widget in flash

Editing Captivate Widgets in Flash

You can edit Captivate Widgets in Flash by loading the fla file in Flash and performing the necessary edits. In this example we will be editing the **Certificate widget** in Flash. This widget is a great tool for those who want to have their students collect a certificate after completing a course. This tutorial is helpful for those who may want to customize the colors, logo and design of the certificate of completion based on the organization's specifications.

1. Navigate to Program Files > Adobe > Adobe Captivate > Gallery > Widgets > Source > **CertificateWidget.fla** and double-click it to open it in Flash.

Important: Save the **fla** file under a new name before you begin editing.

2. The widget loads in Flash. **Locate** the **different styles** of certificates in the library. There is a movie clip for each style. **Choose the style** you want to edit by double-clicking the respective movie clip.

3. **Edit** sections of the certificate, by first **clicking** on the corresponding **layer** in Flash then changing elements in the certificate as desired. You can add text, images, change the position and dimension of fields.

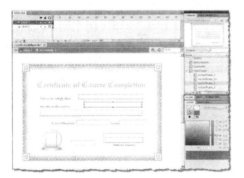

4. **Double-click** sections of the certificate that you would like to edit (or **right click** and choose **Edit Selected**) to dive deeper into the groups of objects. Change colors and design as desired.

5. **Keep double-clicking** to dive deeper into groups of objects, till the object you want to edit is selected. We are going to change the color of the **emblem** in the certificate.

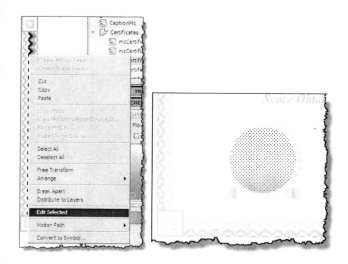

6. Under the **Color** tab, select the desired colors for the gradient in the emblem.

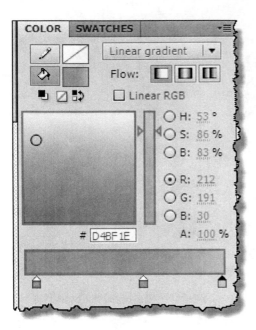

7. The edited emblem with the new colors appears. Repeat the above for other sections of the emblem and other elements of the certificate you would like to edit.

8. The new emblem with name of organization added.

9. The new certificate in Flash after all edits. In this example, we have changed the colors of the border, color of certificate title, colors of the emblem, and added the name of the organization on the emblem.

Certificate of Course Completion

This is to certify that

has taken the course

Score Obtained   *Grade*

XYZ
Company

Authorized Signature

10. Its' time to publish the edited certificate. Click File > Publish

11. Set your Publish Settings including Flash Player version and Action Script version. For use in Captivate 5 and above, this should be ActionScript 3.0.

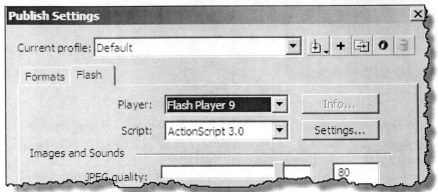

12. Publish your edited Captivate widget with a unique name (e.g. **Certificate Widget_Edited**) in the same folder as the other Captivate widgets: **Program Files > Adobe > Adobe Captivate > Gallery > Widgets**

13. Open Captivate and load the widget window by clicking: Window > Widget. Click the **Refresh** button to load your edited certificate in the list.

14. If your edited certificate does not load, ensure that you have put it in the same directory as the other widgets then click the **Change Path** folder icon and set it to where the widgets are located.

15. The edited certificate widget appears in the list.

16. Insert the Edited certificate unto the stage and in the **Widget Properties** window, from the **Template** drop down list, select the style of certificate you edited in Flash.

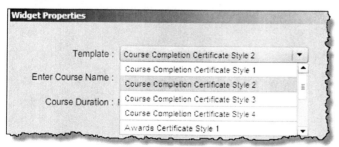

17. Your edited certificate widget is ready for use in Captivate.

Editing Captivate Animations in Flash

You can edit Captivate animations in Flash by loading the fla file in Flash and performing the necessary edits. In this example we will be using the Flash software to edit the **orange_cirlcelight** animation. This animation is a great tool for highlighting sections of your course. This tutorial is helpful for those who may want to change the color and thickness of the animation.

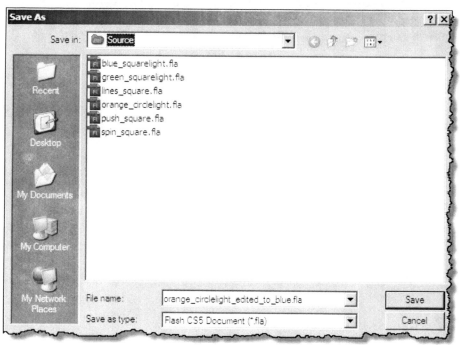

1. Navigate to Program Files > Adobe > Adobe Captivate > Gallery > SWF Animation > Highlights > Source > **orange_circlelight.fla** and double-click it to open it in Flash.

Important: Save the **fla** file under a new name before you begin editing.

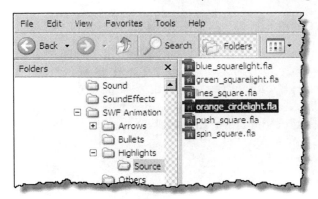

2. The animation loads in Flash. Use the Flash selection tool to select the animation on the stage and double-click it (or **right click** and choose **Edit Selected**) to dive deeper into the groups of objects.

OR

Double-click the **Tween 2** movie clip in the library. Ensure you double-click the icon for the movie clip and not the movie clip name.

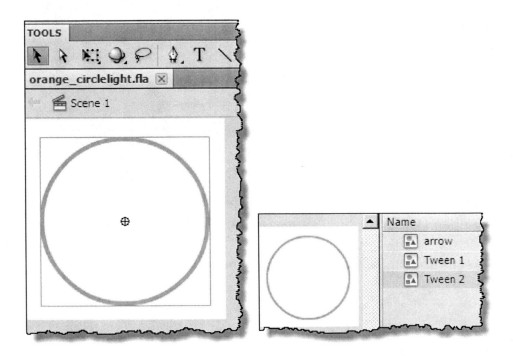

3. The animation opens in a new tab, one level deeper where you can edit its color and width.

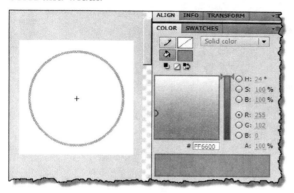

4. Click the Fill Color tool and choose your color of choice for the animation.

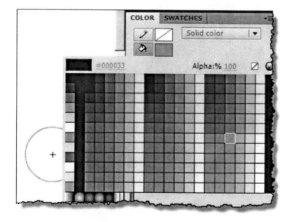

5. We have now changed the animation to blue.

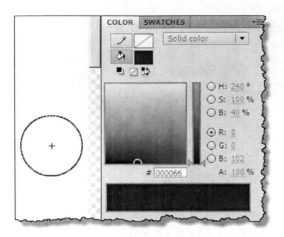

6. The number in the **Stroke** tool controls the thickness of the Stroke in the animation. Increasing this number will make the stroke of the circle animation thicker. Adjust as desired and press **Enter**.

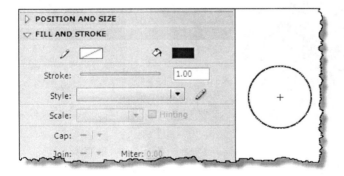

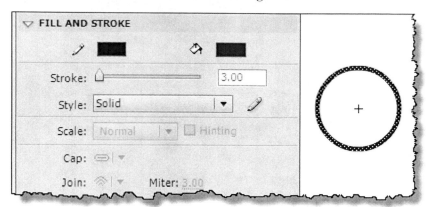

7. The new animation after increasing the thickness of the **Stroke** to **3**.

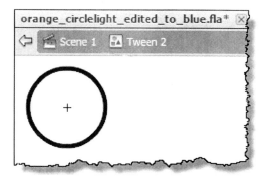

8. Preview the effects of your editing by clicking: **Control > Test Movie > Test**

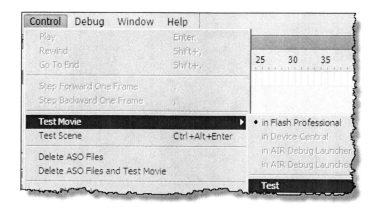

9. It's time to publish the edited animation. Click File > Publish

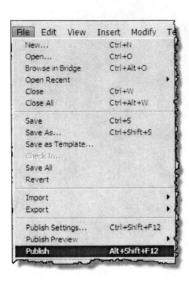

10. Set your Publish Settings including Flash Player version and Action Script version. For use in Captivate 5 and above, this should be ActionScript 3.0.

11. Publish your edited Captivate animation with a unique name (e.g. **orange_circlelight_edited_to_blue.swf**) in the same folder as the other Captivate animations: **Program Files > Adobe > Adobe Captivate > Gallery > SWF Animation > Highlights.**

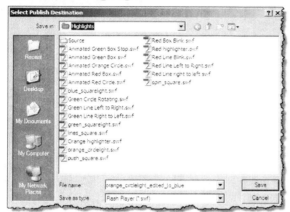

12. To access your edited animation from inside Captivate, click:

Insert > Animation and navigate to where you saved it..

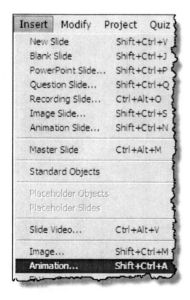

7 – USING WIDGETS

How to Use and Configure Widgets

Use widgets in creative ways to greatly enhance the interactivity and professionalism of your Captivate projects. In this section you will learn how to configure widgets using the Chart widget. The chart and table widgets are excellent for displaying numerical data in interesting and appealing ways.

The Chart Widget

The chart widget allows developers to quickly construct and display attractive charts. You can configure the overall size of the chart, the dimensions of its sections, choose coloring for different sections and add its data. You have the option of building three basic kinds of charts: **Column, Bar** and **Pie charts**.

Constructing Charts

1. To build charts using the charts widget, click **Insert** > **Widget**.

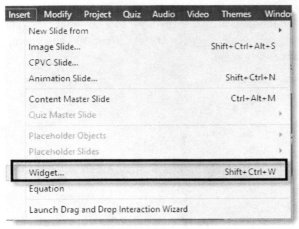

2. Navigate to the location of the widgets: **Program Files** > **Adobe** > **Adobe Captivate 8** > **Gallery** > **Widgets** > **Source** > **ChartsWidget** > **ChartsWidget.swf**.

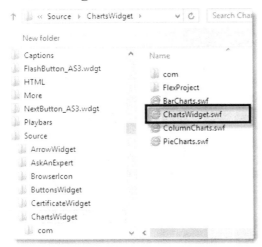

Column, **Bar** or **Pie** chart widgets.

3. The **Widget Properties** window launches. From here, we can choose and configure the types of charts we want to build. Choose the type of Chart: **Column**, **Bar** or **Pie**.

4. For each type, choose the style of chart from the drop-down list. The available styles for Column Charts are: **Clustered**, **Stacked**, **100%** and **Overlaid**.

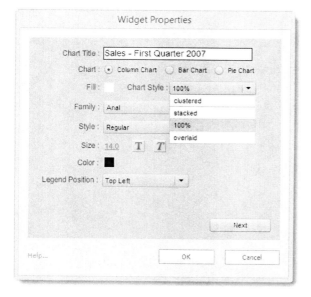

5. Select other properties of the Widget such as, **Fill**, **Font** and **Legend Position**.

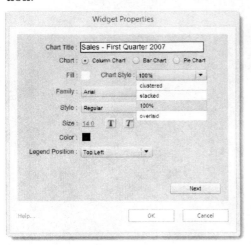

6. Click **Next**.

7. Enter data into chart. **X** Axis = Data. **Y** Axis = Legends.

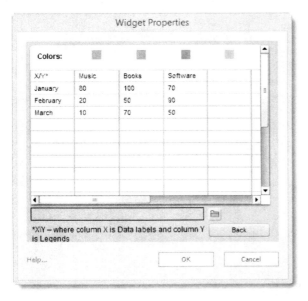

8. Format the **Colors** of the columns.

9. Click **OK**.

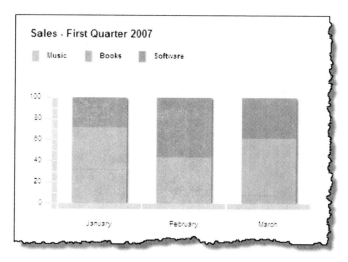

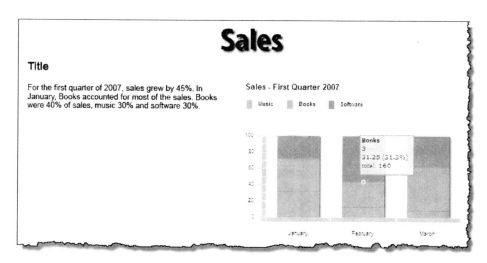

The Chart widget at runtime, displaying sales data for a company that sells music, books and software. The Chart Widgets are interactive and not just static display of information. Rolling the mouse over each color coded section, reveals data for that section.

Formatting Charts

1. Column Charts.

You can configure four types of Column Charts in Captivate: **clustered, stacked, 100%** and **overlaid.**

    1.   To develop a column chart, **click** the **Column Chart** radio button.

2. Click the **Chart Style** drop down menu and select the type of Column chart you want to use.

3. A **Clustered Column** Chart, using the chart widget. The chart is interactive. Rolling the mouse over each color coded section, reveals data for that section.

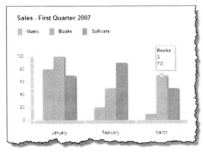

4. A **Stacked Column** Chart from the same data, using the chart widget.

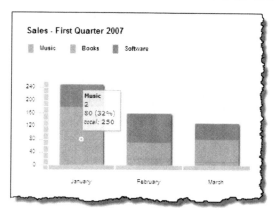

5. A **100% Column** Chart from the same data, using the chart widget. The chart is interactive. Rolling the mouse over each color coded section, reveals data for that section

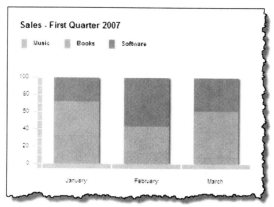

6. An **Overlaid Column** Chart from the same data, using the chart widget. The chart is interactive. Rolling the mouse over each color coded section, reveals data for that section.

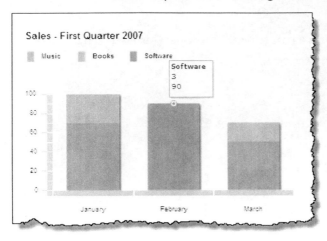

2. Bar Charts

You can configure four types of Bar Charts in Captivate: **clustered**, **stacked**, **100%** and **overlaid**

1. To develop a Bar Chart, **click** the **Bar Chart** radio button.

2. Click the **Chart Style** drop down menu and select the type of Column chart you want to use.

3. A **Clustered Bar** Chart from the same data, using the chart widget. The chart is interactive. Rolling the mouse over each color coded section, reveals data for that section.

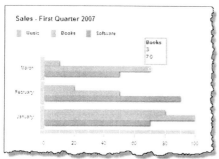

4. A **Stacked Bar** Chart from the same data, using the chart widget.

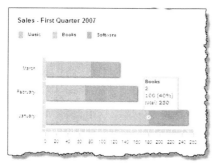

5. A **100% Bar** Chart from the same data, using the chart widget.

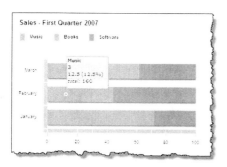

6. An **Overlaid Bar** Chart from the same data, using the chart widget. The charts are interactive. Rolling the mouse over each color coded section, reveals data for that section.

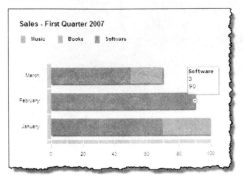

3. Pie Charts

You can configure three types of Bar Charts in Captivate: **regular**, **doughnut** and **exploding.**

1. To develop a Pie Chart, **click** the **Pie Chart** radio button.

2. Click the **Chart Style** drop down menu and select the type of Column chart you want to use.

3. A **Regular Pie** Chart from the same data, using the chart widget.

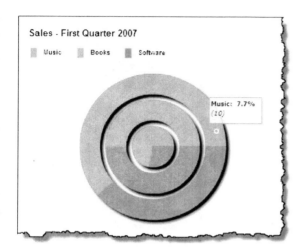

4. A **Doughnut Pie** Chart from the same data, using the chart widget.

5. An **Exploding Pie** Chart from the same data, using the chart widget. The charts are interactive. Rolling the mouse over each color coded section, reveals data for that section.

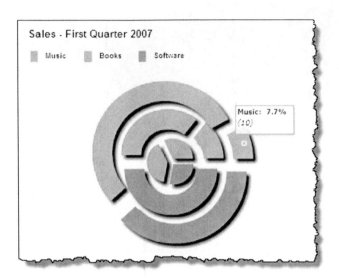

How to Edit Widgets

You can edit Captivate widgets in two ways
1. Exporting the Captivate Project to Flash:
File > Export > To Flash (This exports the entire project to Flash)
2. Open Flash and Load the **fla** file for the widget.

For more information on editing widgets, see the topic in the previous chapter "Editing Captivate Widgets in Flash."

RESOURCES

Working Sample: www.elearnvisual.com/advanced-interactions.html

Captivate source file: www.elearnvisual.com/members.html

(Enter the above URL in your Web browser.)

8 – USING VARIABLES AND ADVANCED ACTIONS

Variables

What is a Variable?

variable is a placeholder or container for information. In Captivate 8, some variables can be stored in text captions while some can be accessed only through advanced actions. **System Variables** are contained within Captivate 8. They can display information about the project or system such as author, project name, slide number, date, time and many more. Some of these variables such as **cpCmnd-ShowPlaybar** and **cpLockTOC** can be manipulated and some cannot. The Captivate developer creates user variables accesses them using text captions and advanced actions. Here is a list of the different categories of system variables.

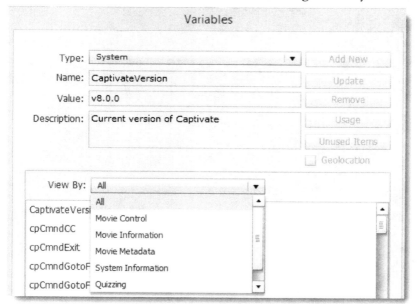

Types of Variables

1. Movie Control Variables

Use advanced actions, widgets and Flash animations to access the variables in this category.

To insert a system variable, first insert a text caption, and then click the insert variable icon.

2. Movie Information Variables:

Access the variables in this category using advanced actions, widgets and Captivate's SWF Components. These variables are stored and displayed via text captions.

Variables	
Type: System ▼	Add New
Name: CaptivateVersion	Update
Value: v8.0.0	Remove
Description: Current version of Captivate	Usage
	Unused Items
	☐ Geolocation

View By: Movie Information ▼

- CaptivateVersion
- cpCmndInfo
- cpInfoCurrentFrame
- cpInfoCurrentSlide
- cpInfoCurrentSlide
- cpInfoCurrentSlideLabel
- cpInfoCurrentSlideType
- cpInfoElapsedTimeMS
- cpInfoFPS

Help...   Close

3. Movie Metadata Variables:

Access the variables in this category using advanced actions, widgets and Captivate's SWF Components. These variables are stored and displayed via text captions.

Variable name	Default value	Description
cpInfoAuthor	author	Name of the author
cpInfoCompany	company	Name of the company
cpInfoCopyright	copyright	Copyright Info
cpInfoCourseID *(New)*	-1	No idea where this comes from
cpInfoCourseName *(New)*	Course Name	No idea where this comes from
cpInfoDescription	project description	Description of the project
cpInfoEmail	author@company.com	e-mail address
cpInfoProjectName		Name of the Adobe Captivate project
cpInfoWebsite	www.company.com	URL of the company website in the format www.companyaddress.com

4. System Information Variables:

You can access the variables in this category using advanced actions, widgets and Captivate's SWF Components.

5. Quizzing Variables:

Access the variables in this category using advanced actions, widgets and Captivate's SWF Components. These variables are stored and displayed via text captions.

In scenarios 2, 3, 4 and 5, you will learn how to create and manipulate these variables to achieve advanced interactivity in Captivate projects.

Advanced Actions

Basic Types of Advanced Actions

Actions in Captivate are based on some event like clicking a button, clicking a click box, entering a slide. Advanced actions allow us to program multiple actions based on one event or a combinations of events. Scripting for advanced actions in Captivate 8 is based on the Object-Event-Action model. Advanced actions allow developers to add more interactivity and control to a Captivate movie using simple scripting with the aid of the Advanced Actions dialog box and Scripting Editor.

Advanced actions in Captivate 8 can take several forms. Here are a few examples:

1. A combination of **standard actions**

2. A conditional action

3. A combination of **standard actions** and **conditional actions**

4. A combination of **variables** and **conditional actions**

5. A combination of **standard actions**, **variables** and **conditional actions**

6. A combination of **widgets** configured by **variables** and **conditional actions**

7. A combination of standard actions, widgets configured by user variables, system variables and conditional actions.

1. A Combination of Standard Actions - Multiple Actions

This kind of advanced action usually takes the form of a combination of standard actions that can be assigned to any button or click box. For example, you can assign four standard actions to the event of one button click: **Show**, **Hide**, **Jump to Slide**, **Add Effect** and **Open File**. What this means is that when the button is clicked, all these actions will be performed in the assigned order. Many combinations are possible, limited only by your imagination. Remember the action of **Add Effect** can add some very creative possibilities to combined standard actions.

The available standard actions for Captivate advanced actions are:

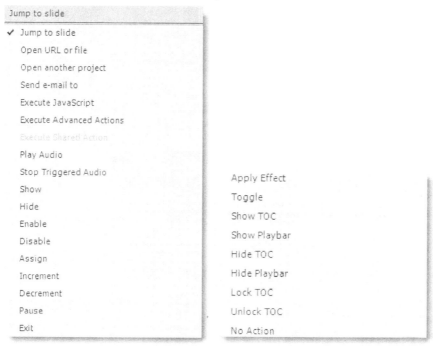

Continue

The user is taken to the next defined action after clicking button.

Go To Previous Slide

The user is taken to the previous slide after clicking button.

Go To Next Slide

The user is taken to the next slide after clicking button.

Go To Last Visited Slide

The user is taken to the previously viewed slide after clicking button.

Return to Quiz

The user is taken back to the last attempted question if it was answered incorrectly.

Jump to Slide

The user is taken to the specified slide after clicking button.

Open URL Or File

After clicking button, the user is taken to a website or file which opens.

Open Other Project

After clicking button, the user is taken to the specified Adobe Captivate project.

Send Mail

After clicking button, the user is taken to the default e-mail editor, which opens with an e-mail draft, addressed" to the recipient as specified.

Execute JavaScript

After the user clicks button, Adobe Captivate executes the specified JavaScript.

Play Audio   A user-click triggers a specified audio file to play

Stop Triggered Audio

After the user clicks the last triggered audio file stops playing

Show

After the user clicks button, the specified hidden object is made visible.

Hide

After the user clicks button, the specified object becomes hidden.

Enable

After the user clicks button, another object in the project is activated.

Disable

After the user clicks button, another object in the project is disabled.

Assign

After the user clicks button, the value of the specified variable is set inside the object.

Increment

Increase the value of a numerical variable.

Decrement

Decrease the value of a numerical variable.

Pause

Pauses the project

Exit

Exits the project

Apply Effect

After the user performs an action, it triggers an effect associated with the object

Expression

Using an expression to change the content of a variable

Toggle

Toggle playbar, TOC or closed captions on or off

Show TOC

Show the Table of Contents

Show Playbar

Show the playbar

Hide TOC

Hide the Table of Contents

Hide Playbar

Hide the playbar

Lock TOC

Lock the Table of Contents from navigation

Unlock TOC

Allow navigation on the Table of Contents

The traditional standard actions: **Execute Advanced Action, Execute Shared Action, No Action** are not available for advanced actions.

2. A Conditional Action - A conditional action has 4 basic parts:

Parts of A Conditional Action

1

DECISION

A **Decision**: The scripting in this section provides the logic for a programming decision to be executed by Captivate. Each Decision has **If**, **Action** and **Else** sections. You can have an Advanced Action with several decisions.

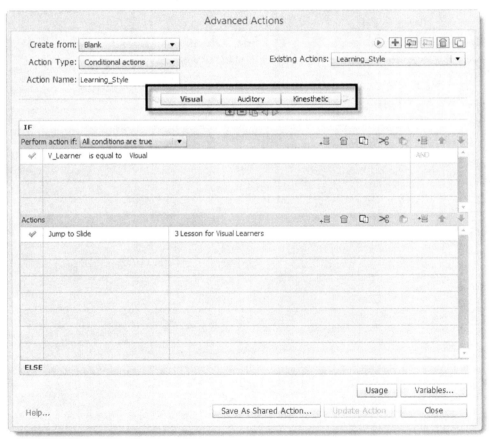

2

IF

The **IF** section provides the condition for executing the advanced action.

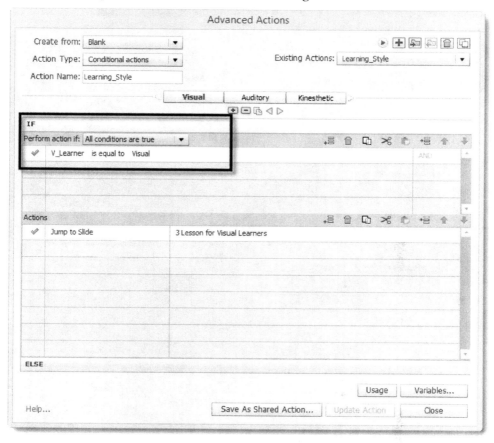

3

ACTIONS

The **Actions** section tells Captivate what to do if the condition is met.

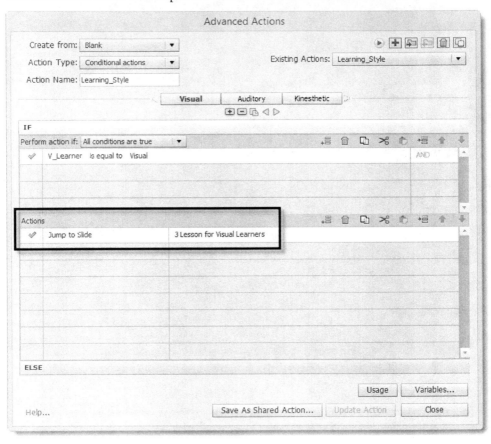

4

ELSE

The **ELSE** section: provides exceptions and limitations for performing the action.

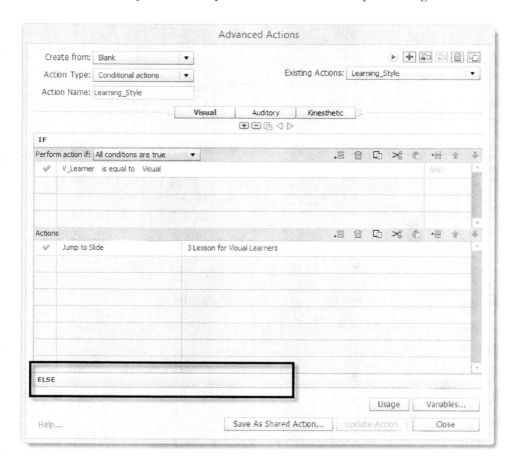

Scripting for Enhanced Interactions

SCENARIO 1 - Clicking Each Image for Information (*Using Multi Standard Actions*)

SCENARIO:

You want users of your course to click several images on a screen, each of which will load specific textual information. You have two images on a screen, one of a laptop and one of a login screen. When the users click each image, textual information for that particular image **only**, appears. You are not forcing the users the view them, as the navigation bar and buttons are available. Users can navigate the course in any order they choose.

THE SOLUTION:

Use an advanced action that combines multi-standard actions. These will be show/hide actions.

WHAT YOU WILL LEARN IN THIS TUTORIAL:

1. How to build an advanced action comprising of multi-standard actions

2. How to use the Show/Hide actions

3. How to use On Enter slide actions.

CREATE CLICK BOXES

STEPS:
CREATE CLICK BOXES

Clicking Each Image for Information > Create Click Boxes

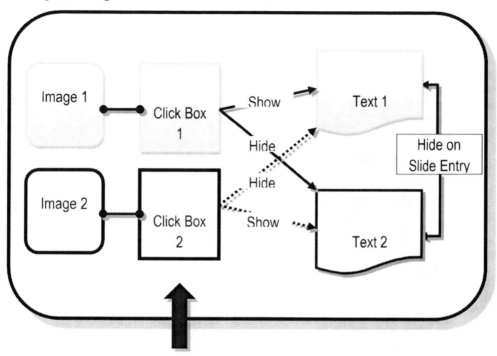

You Are Here

SET UP: Create two **Text Captions**, one for each image. These captions will be the information that is displayed each time a particular image is clicked.

1

Click each image and in the **Item Name** field of the Property Inspector give each a unique name that you can easily identify e.g. Laptop.

2

Insert a **Click Box** over each image.

PROGRAMMING THE ACTION (Show/Hide)

Clicking Each Image for Information > Programming the Action > Show/Hide

1

For each click box, create an **Advanced Action** that will make the relevant text appear when clicked.

Select the **Click Box** over the laptop.

2

In the **Action** area of the Properties panel, Select **Execute Advanced Actions.**

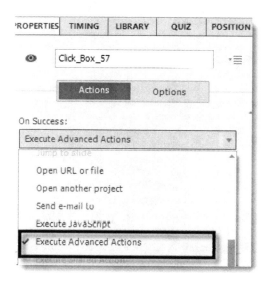

3

Click the **Script** icon.

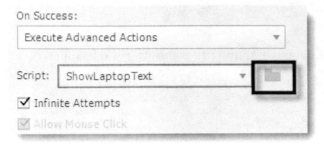

4

In the **Action Type** drop-down menu of the Advanced Actions dialog box, select **Standard Actions.**

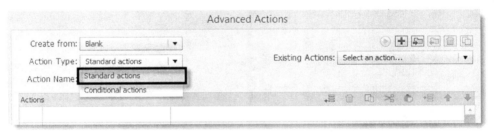

5

In the **Actions** section of the Advanced Actions dialog box, click the **Add** icon.

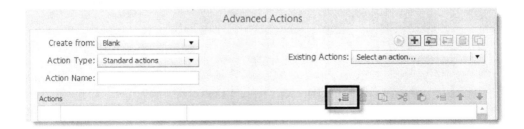

6

Select the **Show** action.

7

Select the object you want to show when the laptop Click Box is clicked. In this case, it's the **Laptop_text.**

8

Click **the line below** and click the **Add** icon to add a Hide action.

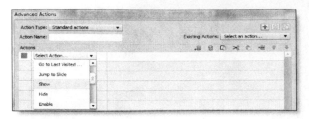

Clicking Each Image for Information > Programming the Action > Show/Hide

9

Select the **Hide** action.

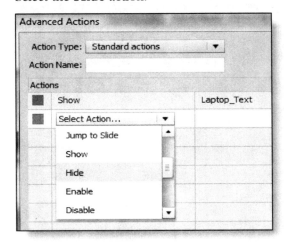

10

Select the object you want to show when the laptop Click Box is clicked. In this case, it's the **Login_text.**

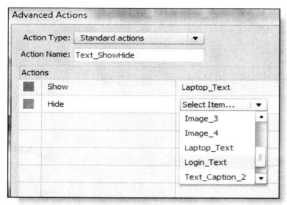

Clicking Each Image for Information > Programming the Action > Show/Hide

11

Give your Advanced Action a **Name.**

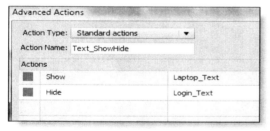

12

Click **Save.**

13

Repeat the above steps for click box over the other image. In this instance, **reverse** the show hide actions to Hide the **Laptop_Text** and Show the **Login_Text.**

NOTE: You have just programmed Captivate to show the Laptop_Text when the laptop image is clicked and to show the Login_Text when the login image is clicked.

ON SLIDE ENTRY

Clicking Each Image for Information > Programming the Action > On Slide Entry

1

Click on the slide with the Advanced Actions you just programmed.

2

In the Property Inspector, under the Action area, in the On Enter drop-down menu, select **Execute Advanced Actions.**

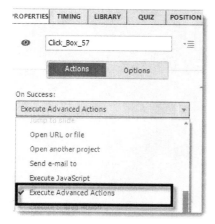

3

Click the **Script** icon.

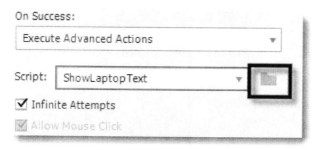

4

In the Advanced Actions dialog box click the plus **(+)** sign to create a **new Advanced Action**.

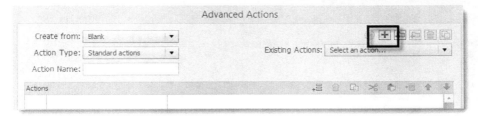

5

In the **Action Type** drop-down menu, select **Standard actions.**

6

Give your Advanced Action a **name.**

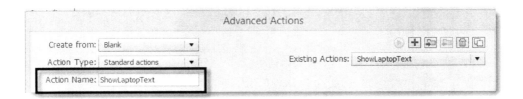

7

Click the **Add** Icon.

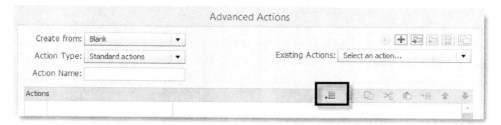

8

Select the **Hide** action.

9

Select the items you want to hide on slide entry: Select the **Laptop Text.**

10

Click **Save / Update.**

11

Repeat the above steps for the **Login_Text**.

NOTE: You have just programmed Captivate to hide the Laptop and Login Text when a user enters the slide.

RESOURCES

Working Sample: www.elearnvisual.com/advanced-interactions.html

Captivate source file: www.elearnvisual.com/members.html

(Enter the above URL in your Web browser.)

SCENARIO 2 - Clicking Each Image for Information with Navigation Control (*Using Conditional Actions with Multi Standard Actions and User Variables*).

SCENARIO:

You want users of your course to click all images on a screen before proceeding to the next page. You have information the users need to read before accessing courses on the LMS. You have two images on a screen, one of a laptop and one of a login screen. When the users click each image, textual information for that particular image **only**, appears. The users will not be allowed to proceed to the next screen until they have clicked all images. A Continue button will appear only after they have clicked both the laptop and login images.

THE SOLUTION:

Use an **Advanced Action** that combines multi-standard actions with a conditional action that checks to see if the user clicked all images. Use an advanced action that combines multi-hide actions on slide entry.

WHAT YOU WILL LEARN IN THIS TUTORIAL:

1. How to build an advanced action comprising of multi-standard actions

2. How to build a conditional action

3. How to use the Show/Hide actions

4. How to use On Enter slide actions.

5. How to create user variables

6. How to associate variables with objects using advanced actions

7. How to control user navigation using advanced actions

DESIGN MAP - CREATE CLICK BOXES AND USER VARIABLES
STEPS:

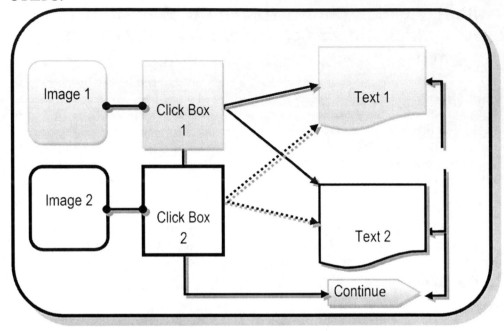

CREATE CLICK BOXES AND USER VARIABLES

Clicking Each Image for Information > Create Click Boxes and User Variables

1

Click each image and in the **Item Name** field of the Properties panel give the image a unique name that you can easily identify e.g. Laptop.

2

Insert a **Click Box** over each image.

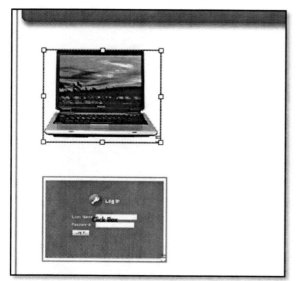

3 Create **user variables** to associate with the click boxes.

3A

Click **Project** > **Variables.**

3B

Select **User** in the Type drop-down menu.

3C

Click **Add New.**

3D

Give your variable a **Name**. We'll call it HitOne.

3E

Give it a value of **0.**

3F

Give it a **description**.

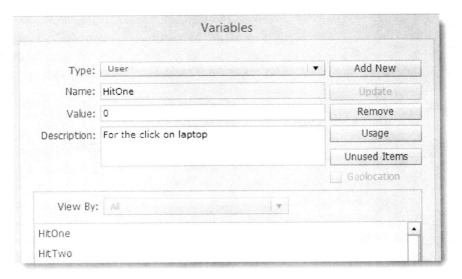

3G

Click **Save.**

3H

Do the above for another user variable, naming it HitTwo.

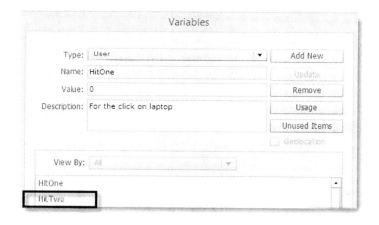

NOTE: You have now created two user variables with a value of 0: HitOne and HitTwo.

ADVANCED ACTION – DECISION 1 (Assigning User Variables to Click Boxes)

For each click box, create an advanced action that will make the relevant text appear when clicked and the continue button appear after all images are clicked:

SETTING THE CONDITION

Decision 1 > Assign User Variables to Click Boxes > Setting the Condition

SET UP: Create two **Text Captions**, one for each image. These captions will be the information that will be displayed when the user clicks each image.

1

Insert a **Click Box** over each image.

2

Select the **Click Box** over the laptop.

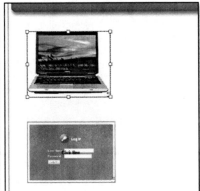

3

Under Action area of the Properties panel, select **Execute Advanced Actions.**

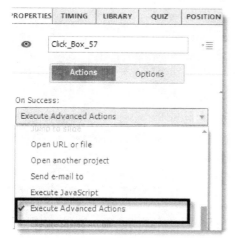

4

Click the **Script** icon

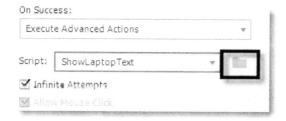

5

In the **Action Type** drop-down menu, select **Conditional actions.**

179

6

Double click the first **decision tab** and label it Decision 1. Remember conditional actions are decisions that specify a series of actions to be taken based on an If condition. An advanced action can have several decisions.

7

In the **IF** section, click the drop-down menu under **Perform action if**, and select **All conditions are true**. This programs the click box to perform a certain action or actions if the conditions you are about to specify are met.

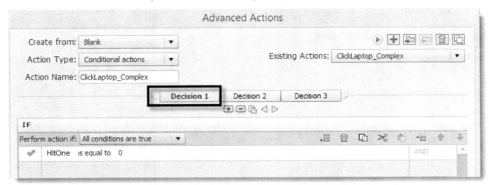

8

Click the **Add** icon.

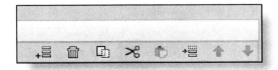

9

Select **variable.**

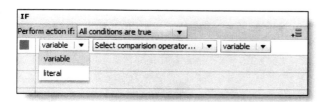

10

Choose the **HitOne** user variable you created earlier. What you are doing here is associating HitOne variable with the click box over the laptop.

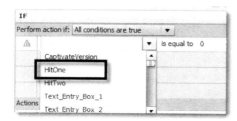

11

Select **is equal to** as the comparison operator.

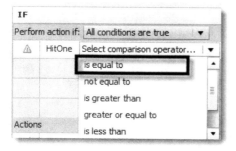

12

Choose between **Variable** and **Literal**. Select **Literal**. If you make a mistake, it's easier to start over.

13

Give it a value of **0**.

NOTE: What you have just programmed is every time the laptop click box is clicked it calls the HitOne variable which has a value of 0. You are further implying if HitOne has a value of 0, to perform some kind of action. Let's program the action.

PROGRAMMING THE ACTION

Decision 1 > Assign User Variables to Click Boxes > Programming the Action

1

Under the Actions section of the **Advanced Actions** dialog box, click the **Add** icon to add an action.

2

Select the action you want to execute. In this case, choose **Assign.**

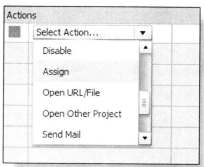

3

Select the **HitOne** variable.

4

Choose between **Variable** and **Literal**. Select **Literal**.

5

Give it a value of **1**.

6

Give your advanced action a **name.**

7

Click **Save** and close.

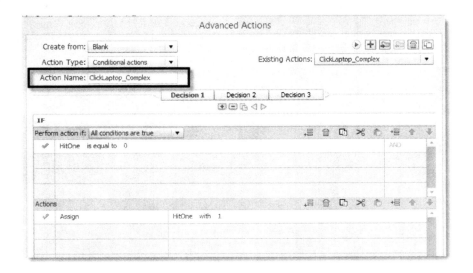

NOTE: What you have just programmed is anytime the Click Box over the laptop is clicked, call the HitOne variable which has a value of 0 and assign the variable a literal value of 1. This is Decision 1. We will create 2 more Decisions for this Click Box.

ADVANCED ACTION - DECISION 2 (Making the Continue Button Appear After Both Click Boxes Are Clicked)

SETTING THE CONDITION

Decision 2 > Making the Continue Button Appear > Setting the Condition

1

Double click the second **decision tab** and label it **Decision 2**.

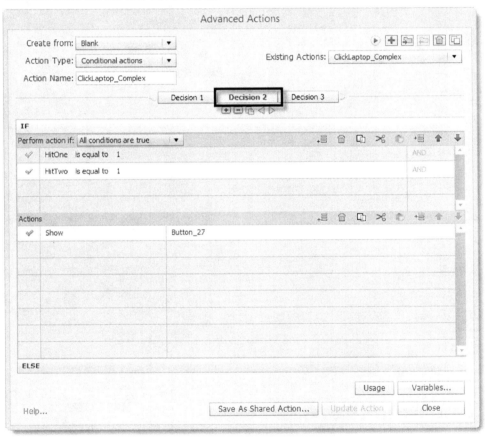

2

Under the **IF** section, click the drop-down menu under **Perform action if**, and select **All conditions are true**. This programs the click box to perform a certain action or actions if the conditions you are about to specify are met.

3

Click the **Add** icon.

4

Select **variable.**

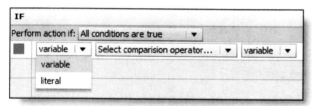

5

Choose the **HitOne** user variable you created earlier.

6

Select **is equal to** as the comparison operator.

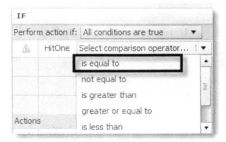

7

Choose between **Variable** and **Literal**. Select **Literal**. If you make a mistake, it's easier to start over.

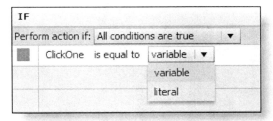

8

Give it a value of **1**.

> **NOTE**: What you have done so far is to establish a condition that every time the HitOne variable acquires a value of 1 (It changes from **0** to **1** every time the laptop Click Box is clicked), some action should be performed.

9

Repeat steps 1 to 9 for the HitTwo variable.

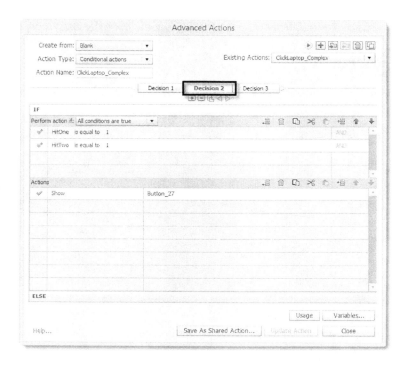

NOTE: What you about to program is every time the HitOne variable acquires a value of 1 (It changes from 0 to 1 every time the laptop Click Box is clicked) AND the HitTwo variable acquires a value of 1, (It changes from 0 to 1 every time the login Click Box is clicked), when both these conditions are met, some action should be performed. Let's program the action.

PROGRAMMING THE ACTION

Decision 2 > Making the Continue Button Appear > Programming the Action

1

Under the **Actions** section of the Advanced Actions dialog box, click the **Add** icon to add an action.

2

Select the action you want to execute. In this case, choose **Show**

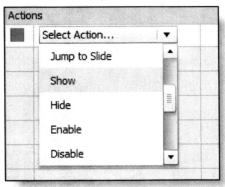

3

Select the Object you want to show when both conditions are met. In this case, we choose **Continue**. This Continue button will take the user to the next screen.

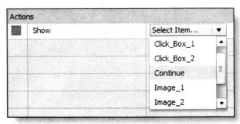

4

Click **Update**.

NOTE: What you have just programmed is every time the HitOne variable acquires a value of 1 (It changes from **0** to **1** every time the laptop Click Box is clicked) AND the HitTwo variable acquires a value of **1**, (It changes from **0** to **1** every time the login Click Box is clicked), when both these conditions are met, show the Continue button. Adding an action to show the Continue button assumes it is hidden. We will see later how to hide the Continue button.

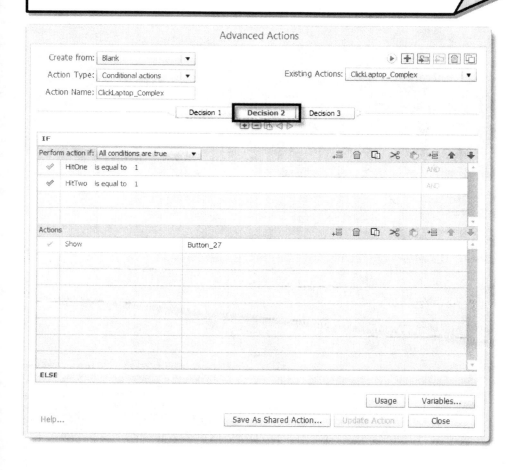

ADVANCED ACTION - DECISION 3 (Making Relevant Text Appear when a Click Box is Clicked)

Decision 3 > Making Relevant Text Appear > Setting the Condition

1 Double click the third **decision tab** and label it **Decision 3**.

2

Click the **Add** icon.

3

Select **variable.**

4

Choose the HitOne user variable you created earlier.

5

Select **is equal to** as the comparison operator.

6

Choose between **Variable** and **Literal**. Select **Literal**. If you make a mistake choosing the wrong option, it's easier to start over.

7

Give it a value of **1**.

NOTE: What you have done so far is to establish a condition that every time the HitOne variable acquires a value of **1** (It changes from **0** to **1** every time the laptop Click Box is clicked), some action should be performed.

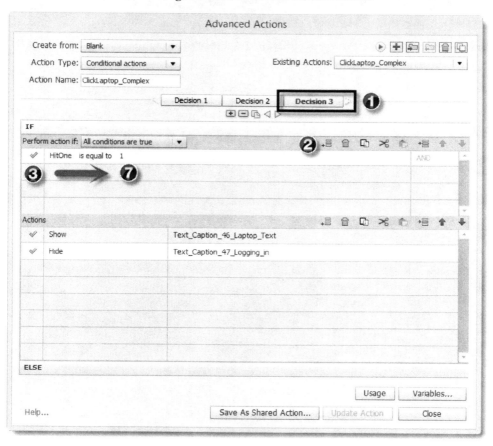

What you about to program is every time the HitOne variable acquires a value of **1** (It changes from **0** to **1** every time the laptop Click Box is clicked) some action should be performed. In **Decision 3**, it will be a show/hide action for the two text objects. Let's program the action.

PROGRAMMING THE ACTION

Decision 3 > Making Relevant Text Appear > Programming the Action

1

Under the Actions section of the Advanced dialog box, click the Add icon to add an action.

2

Select the action you want performed. In this case, choose **Show**

3

Select the Object you want to show when the condition of clicking the Click Box is met. In this case, we choose **Text_Laptop**.

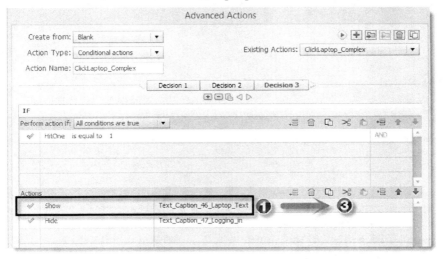

NOTE: What you have just programmed is every time the HitOne variable acquires a value of 1 (It changes from 0 to 1 every time the laptop Click Box is clicked) show the laptop text. Let's program a hide action.

4

Under the Actions section of the Advanced dialog box, click the Add icon to add an action.

5

Select the action you want performed. In this case, choose **Hide.**

6

Select the Object you want to Hide when the condition of clicking the Click Box is met. In this case, we choose **Text_Login.**

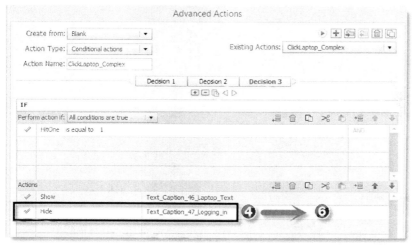

7

Click **Update.**

NOTE: What you have just programmed is every time the HitOne variable acquires a value of 1 (It changes from 0 to 1 every time the laptop Click Box is clicked) show the laptop text and hide the login text.

PROGRAMMING CLICKBOX 2

Repeat the above steps to add the advanced action for the **Click Box over the laptop**. Your advanced actions should look like this:

Decision 1

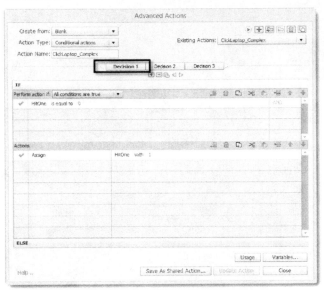

Decision 3

The difference in Decision 3 is that you will **reverse** the Show/hide action: show the Login text and hide the Laptop text.

HIDE ACTION ON SLIDE ENTRY

Clicking Each Image for Info > Hide Action on Slide Entry

1

Click on the slide with the advanced actions you just programmed.

2

In the **Action** area of the Properties panel, and in the **On Enter** drop-down menu, select **Execute Advanced Actions.**

3

Click the **Script** icon.

4

In the Action Type drop-down menu, select **Standard actions.**

5

Name your **Advanced Action**.

6

Click the **Add** Icon.

7

Select the **Hide** action.

8

Select the item you want to hide on slide entry: Select the **Continue** Button.

9

Click **Save**.

10

On returning to the stage, ensure that your new advanced action is selected. You need to do this every time you create an advanced action and exit the **Advanced Actions** dialog box.

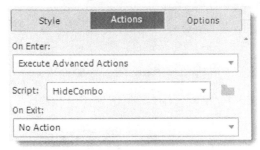

Repeat the above steps for the Logging in and Laptop text captions.

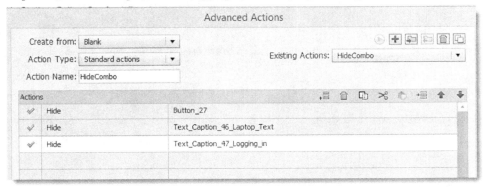

NOTE: You have just programmed Captivate to hide the Continue button and text captions on slide entry. The text captions will be shown only when the user clicks the relevant click boxes (A click box is over each image). The continue button will be shown only when the conditions of clicking all the images are met, allowing the user to proceed.

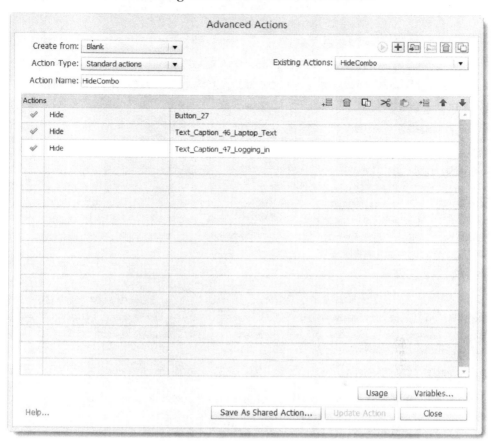

RESOURCES

Working Sample: www.elearnvisual.com/advanced-interactions.html

Captivate source file: www.elearnvisual.com/members.html

(Enter the above URL in your Web browser.)

SCENARIO 3 - Navigation Completely Disabled until All Objects Are Clicked (Using Conditional Actions with Multi Standard Actions, System Variables and User Variables)

SCENARIO:

You want users of your course to click all images on a screen before proceeding to the next page. You have information the users need to read before using an LMS. You have two images on a screen, one of a laptop and one of a login screen. When the users click each image, textual information for that particular image **only**, appears. The users will not be allowed to proceed to the next screen until they have clicked all images. A continue button will appear only after they have clicked both the laptop and login images.

IN ADDITION

Your module has a playbar at the bottom of each screen. You do not want users to skip the interaction on this particular screen by clicking the forward button on the playbar. You would like the playbar to disappear on this screen and re-appear only after users have clicked all images.

THE SOLUTION:

Use an **Advanced Action** that combines multi-standard actions with a conditional action that checks to see if the user has clicked all images. Use an advanced action that combines multi-hide actions on slide entry.

Manipulate a system variable that controls the appearance and disappearance of the playbar.

WHAT YOU WILL LEARN IN THIS TUTORIAL:

1. How to build an advanced action comprising of multi-standard actions

2. How to build a conditional action

3. How to use the Show/Hide actions

4. How to use On Enter slide actions.

5. How to create user variables

6. How to manipulate system variables

7. How to associate variables with objects using advanced actions

8. How to control user navigation using advanced actions and system variables

CREATE CLICK BOXES AND USER VARIABLES

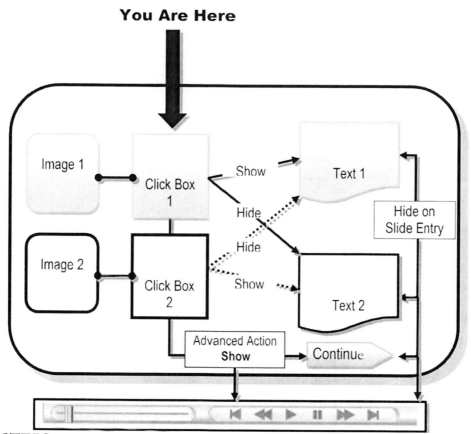

STEPS:

1. Follow the steps outlined in the previous scenario for creating the click boxes and variables for each image and creating the Show/Hide advanced actions for the text objects and continue button.

2. The additional steps for this scenario are for creating the advanced actions for hiding and revealing the Captivate playbar after all objects are clicked. This will require an extra Decision tab in the Advanced actions pane.

ADVANCED ACTION - DECISION 4 (Making the Playbar Appear after All Clicks)

SETTING THE CONDITION

Decision 4 > Making the Playbar Appear > Setting the Condition

1

Click the **(+)** sign to add a fourth Decision tab.

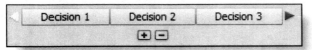

2

Double click the **fourth decision tab** and label it **Decision 4.**

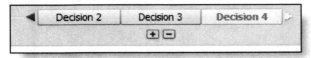

3

Under the IF section, click the drop-down menu under Perform action if, and select **All conditions are true**. This programs the click box to perform a certain action or actions if the conditions you are about to specify are met.

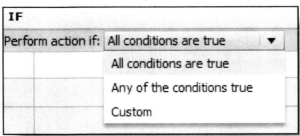

4 Click the Add icon.

5

Select **variable**.

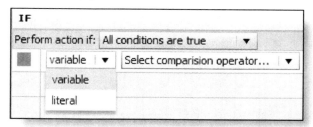

6

Choose the **TotalHits** user variable you created earlier.

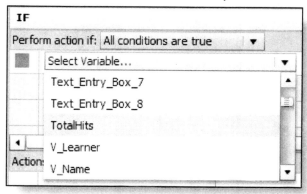

7

Select **is equal to** as the comparison operator.

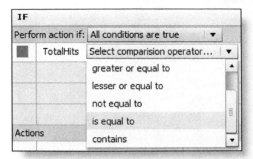

8

Choose between Variable and Literal. Select **Literal**. If you erroneously select the wrong item in this dropdown list, it's easier to delete the action in this line and start over.

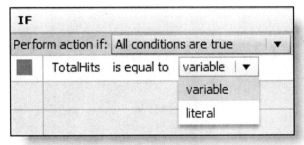

9

Give it a value of **2**.

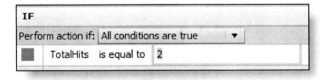

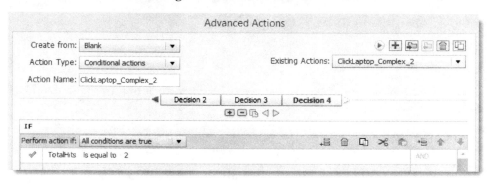

What you about to program is that action. In Decision 4, it will be making the playbar re-appear. Making the playbar re-appear, assumes it is hidden. Later we will see how to hide the playbar. For now, let's program the action to make it appear after being hidden.

PROGRAMMING THE ACTION

1

Under the Actions section of the Advanced dialog box, click the **Add** icon to add an action.

2

Select the action you want performed. In this case, choose **ShowPlaybar**

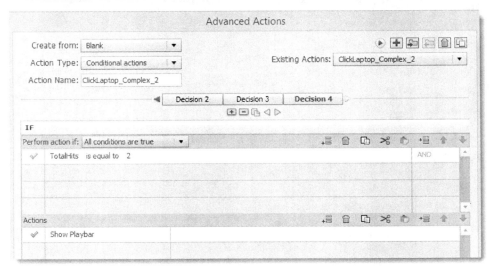

3

Click **Update**.

HIDE ACTION ON SLIDE ENTRY

Decision 4 > Hide Action on Slide Entry > Texts, Button and Playbar

1

Click on the slide with the advanced actions you just programmed.

2

In the **Action** area of the Properties panel, and in the **On Enter** drop-down menu, select **Execute Advanced Actions.**

3

Click the **Script** icon.

4

In the Action Type drop-down menu, select **Standard actions.**

5

Name your **Advanced Action**.

6

Click the **Add** Icon.

7

Select the **Hide** action.

8

Select the item you want to hide on slide entry: Select the **Continue** Button.

9

Click **Save**.

10

On returning to the stage, ensure that your new advanced action is selected. You need to do this every time you create an advanced action and exit the **Advanced Actions** dialog box.

11

Repeat the above steps for **Laptop text**, and **Login text**. Add the **Hide Playbar** action.

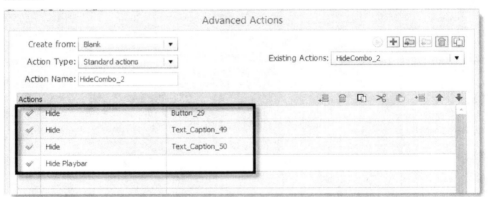

RESOURCES

Working Sample: www.elearnvisual.com/advanced-interactions.html

Captivate source file: www.elearnvisual.com/members.html (Enter URL in your Web browser).

SCENARIO 4 - A Personalized and Customized Course Based on a Personality Assessment *(Using Conditional Actions with User Variables and Widgets)*

SCENARIO:

You would like your courses to have that personal touch for the user. Occasionally, you would like to address the user by first name. You would also like to customize the content and presentation of the course based on a user's learning style. You would like to customize the course based on three learning styles: Visual, Auditory and Kinesthetic.

THE SOLUTION

Create user variables that store the participant's name and learning style. Create advanced actions that will program the customizing of content based on learner style.

WHAT YOU WILL LEARN IN THIS TUTORIAL

1. How to create user variables

2. How to use widgets

3. How to associate variables with widgets using advanced actions

4. How to control user navigation using advanced actions and system variables

5. How to customize course content depending on user input

STEPS - 5 BASIC STEPS

1. Create an entry slide where you will collect user information

2. Insert a Text Entry Box and User Variable to collect the user's name

3. Add a Drop-down widget and User variable to collect the user's learning style

4. Add extra Slides for response and custom courses

5. Add variables and advanced actions on second slide.

Let us look at them in more detail.

CREATE AND PROGRAM ENTRY SLIDE

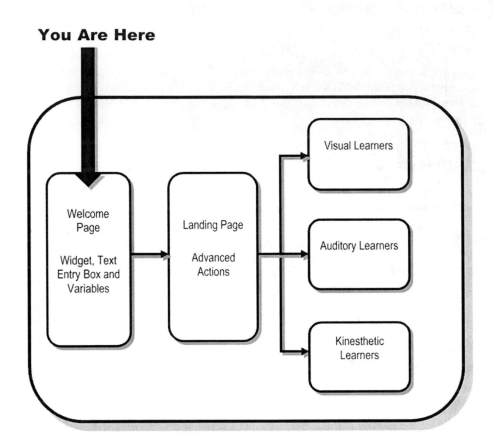

CREATE AND PROGRAM ENTRY SLIDE

1

Create an **entry slide** where you will collect user information.

Add any **caption** that will guide the user.

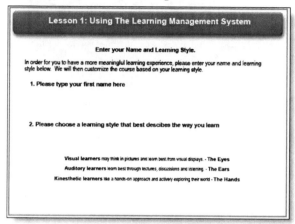

2

Insert a **Text Entry Box** and **User Variable** to collect the user's name.

2A.

Click **Text > Text Entry Box**. We will use it to collect the user's first name.

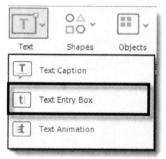

2B

De-select:

Retain Text,

Validate User Input.

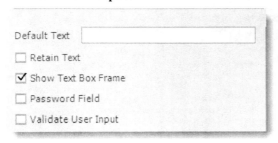

2C

In the **Action** area set:

On Success - Go to next slide.

Attempts - Infinite

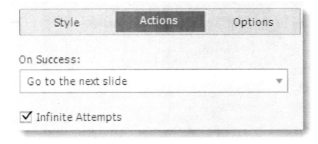

2D

In the **Display** section, check: **Hint.** In the **Others** section, check **Show button.**

2E

With the Text Entry Box selected, type a **name for the variable** (Project > Varia-bles) to associate with the text entry box. We'll call it **V_Name.**

2F

Click on **the button associated with the Text Entry Box**. Change the **Button Type** to Text Button with the text **Submit**.

The user will click this button after entering name and learning style. We will add advanced actions to this button later. This button will navigate the user to different paths in the module depending on their input.

3

Add a **dropdown widget** and User variable to collect the user's learning style.

3A

Add a **dropdown** widget to the stage (Project > Widget > Program Files > Adobe > Adobe Captivate 8 > Gallery > Widgets > Source > dropdown.swf. The Widget Properties dialog box opens up.

3B

In the **Widget Properties** dialog box, enter the values for the Widget. These will be the three different learning styles: **Visual, Auditory,** and **Kinesthetic** - separated by commas.

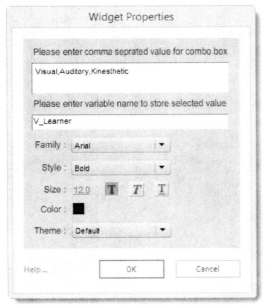

3C

Enter a **name** for the variable associated with the Widget - **V_Learner**.

3D

Choose **other properties** of the Widget such as font.

And Click **OK**.

4

Add **extra slides** for feedback texts and custom courses.

This course will use branching scenarios - a path of slides for each learning style. For this tutorial, we will create just 4 extra slides. Just remember, if in reality we are going to build a course of this complexity, it will consist of many slides, a group for each learning style.

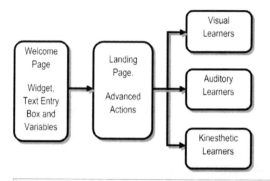

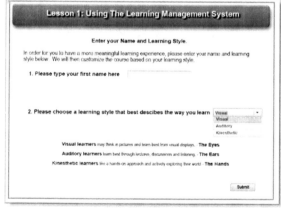

5

Add a **landing page** and content slides.

5A

Create a **landing page** to which users will navigate, after clicking the Submit button on the first page. The Next button on the landing page will have advanced actions that will direct the user to a path for either Visual Learners, Auditory Learners or Kinesthetic Learners.

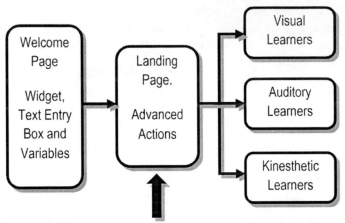

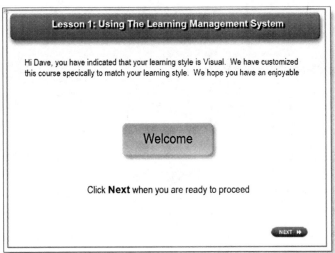

5B

Create a **page for Visual Learners**. All other slides linked to this page should contain content specifically designed for visual learners.

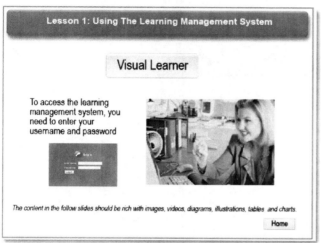

5C

C. Create a page for **Auditory Learners**. All other slides linked to this page should contain content specifically designed for Auditory learners

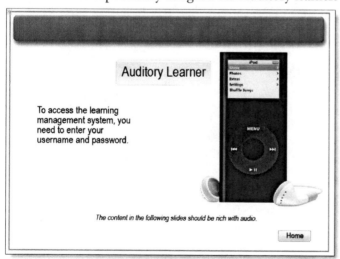

5D

A page for **Kinesthetic Learners**. All other slides linked to this page should contain content specifically designed for visual learners.

Now it's time to program everything to work with some scripting. We will use a combination of advanced actions.

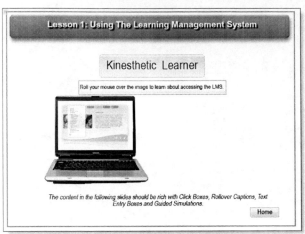

PROGRAMMING THE ACTION

We will use variables and advanced actions on the second slide.

THE VARIABLES

Here, we add some captions to address the user, calling the variables we used on the first page that collected the person's first name and learning style.

The caption inside Captivate will look something like:

Hi $$V_Name$$, you have indicated that your learning style is $$V_Learner$$. We have customized this course specially to match your learning style. We hope you have an enjoyable learning experience. Click Next to continue.

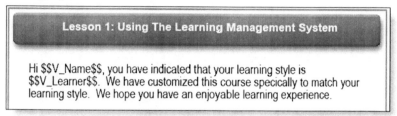

So if a person enters a first name of **Dave** with an **Auditory** Learning style on the first page, this is how it will look at run time on the second page:

*Hi **Dave**, you have indicated that your learning style is **Auditory**. We have customized this course specially to match your learning style. We hope you have an enjoyable learning experience. Click Next to continue.*

ADDING THE VARIABLES

Customized Course Based on Personality Assessment > Adding the Variables

1

Insert a **Text Caption** with words that welcome the user and call the **V_Name** and **V_Learner** user variables we created earlier.

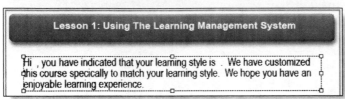

2

After typing "HI", Click the **Insert Variable icon** under the **Character** section of the Properties tab.

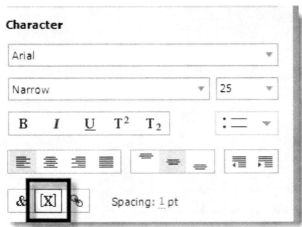

3

Under the Variable Type drop-down menu, select **User**.

4

Under the Variables drop-down menu, select **V_Name.**

5

Click **OK**. Now the user will be addressed by their first name, wherever in the course you use the V_Name variable.

6

After typing **"learning style is"** click the **Insert Variable icon** under the Format tab.

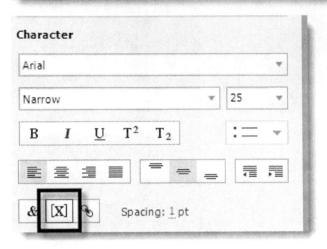

7

Under the Variable Type drop-down menu, select **User**.

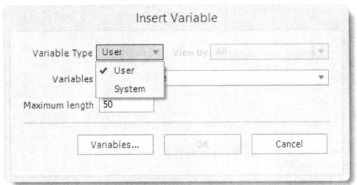

8

Under the Variables drop-down menu, select **V_Learner**.

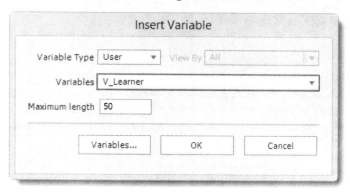

9

Click **OK**. That's it! Now let's program the advanced actions

ADDING THE ADVANCED ACTIONS

ADVANCED ACTION - DECISION 1 (Visual Learners)

Create a **Next button** on the same page (second page) where the above variables are called. We are going to add some advanced actions to this button that will direct Visual Learners to the Visual Learning pages, Auditory Learners to the Auditory Learning pages and Kinesthetic Learners to the pages customized for kinesthetic learners.

SETTING THE CONDITION

Decision 1 > Setting the Condition > For Visual Learners

1

Click the **Next button.**

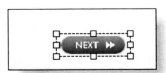

2

Under the Action area of the Properties panel and in the On Success drop-down menu, Select **Execute Advanced Actions.**

3

Click the **Script** icon.

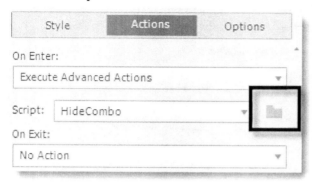

4

In the Advanced Actions dialog box click the plus (**+**) sign to create a new advanced action.

5

In the Action Type drop-down menu, select **Conditional actions**.

6

Double click the **first decision tab** and label it **Visual**. Remember conditional actions are decisions that specify a series of actions to be taken based on a condition. An advanced action can have several decisions.

7

Under the IF section, click the **drop-down menu** under Perform action if, and select **All conditions are true**. This programs the button to perform a certain action or actions if the conditions you are about to specify are met.

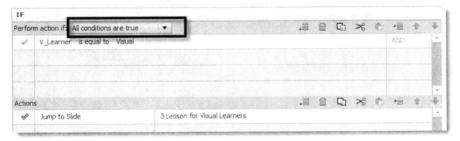

8

Click the **Add icon** and Select **variable.**

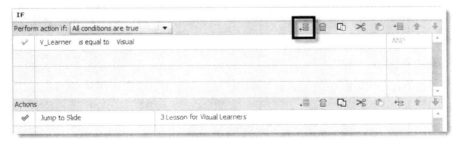

9

Choose the **V_Learner** user variable you created earlier.

10

Select **is equal to** as the comparison operator.

11

Choose between **Variable** and **Literal**. Select **Literal**.

12

Give it a value of **Visual**.

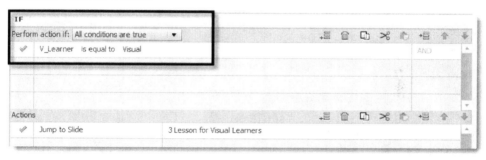

NOTE: What you have just programmed is every time the Next Button is clicked it calls the V_Learner variable. You are further saying if V_Learner variable has a value of Visual, to perform some kind of action. Let's program the action.

PROGRAMMING THE ACTION

1

Under the **Actions** section of the Advanced dialog box, click the **Add icon** to add an action.

2

Select **the action** you want performed. In this case, choose **Jump to Slide**.

3

Select the **slide prepared for visual learners**.

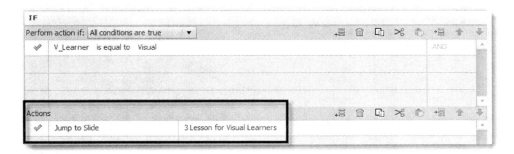

4

Give your advanced action a **name**.

5

Click **Save**.

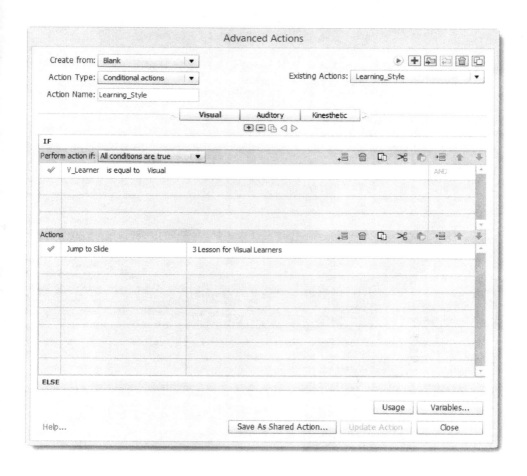

NOTE: What you have just programmed is every time the Next Button is clicked it calls the V_Learner variable. You are further saying if V_Learner variable has a value of Visual, to jump to the entry slide for visual learners.

ADVANCED ACTION - DECISION 2 (Auditory Learners)

SETTING THE CONDITION

1

With the Advanced Actions dialog box still open, double click the **second decision tab** and label it **Auditory**.

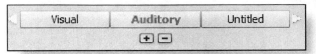

2

Under the IF section, click the **drop-down menu** under Perform action if, and select **All conditions are true**. This programs the button to perform a certain action or actions if the conditions you are about to specify are met.

3

Click the **Add icon.**

4

Select **variable**.

5

Choose the **V_Learner** user variable you created earlier.

6

Select **is equal to** as the comparison operator.

7

Choose between **Variable** and **Literal**. Select **Literal**. If you make a mistake, it's easier to start over.

8

Give it a value of **Auditory**.

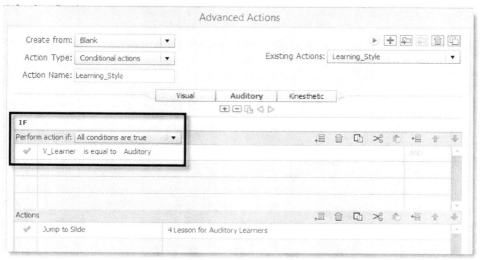

NOTE: What you have just programmed is every time the Next Button is clicked it calls the V_Learner variable. You are further saying if V_Learner variable has a value of Auditory, to perform some kind of action. Let's program the action.

PROGRAMMING THE ACTION

1

Under the Actions section of the Advanced dialog box, click the **Add icon** to add an action.

2

Select the **action** you want performed. In this case, choose **Jump to Slide**.

3

Select the **slide prepared for Auditory learners.**

4

Click **Update**.

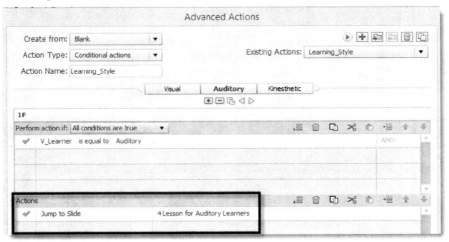

NOTE: What you have just programmed is every time the Next Button is clicked it calls the V_Learner variable. You are further saying if V_Learner variable has a value of Auditory, to jump to the entry slide for auditory learners.

ADVANCED ACTION - DECISION 3 (Kinesthetic Learners)

SETTING THE CONDITION

1

With the Advanced Actions dialog box still open, double click **the third decision tab** and label it **Kinesthetic**.

2

Under the IF section, click **the drop-down menu** under Perform action if, and select **All conditions are true**. This programs the button to perform a certain action or actions if the conditions you are about to specify are met.

3

Click the **Add icon**.

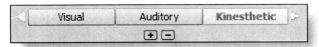

4

Select variable.

5

Choose the **V_Learner** user variable you created earlier.

6

Select **variable**.

7

Give it a value of **Kinesthetic**.

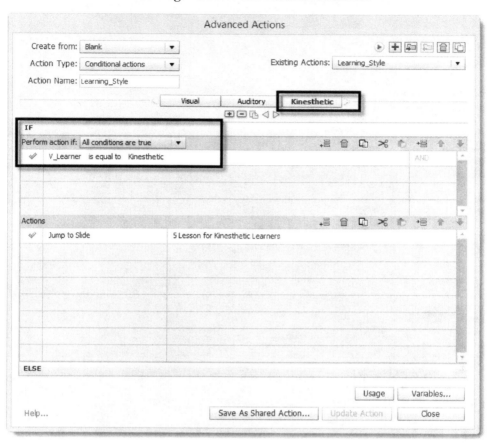

NOTE: What you have just programmed is every time the Next Button is clicked it calls the V_Learner variable. You are further saying if V_Learner variable has a value of Kinesthetic, to perform some kind of action. Let's program the action.

PROGRAMMING THE ACTION

1

Under the Actions section of the Advanced dialog box, click the **Add icon** to add an action.

2

Select the action you want performed. In this case, choose **Jump to Slide**.

3

Select the **slide prepared for Kinesthetic learners**.

4

Click **Update.**

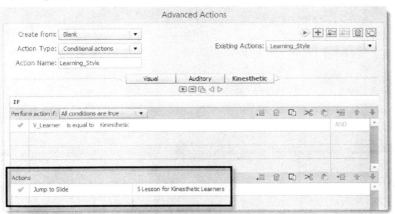

NOTE: What you have just programmed is every time the Next Button is clicked it calls the V_Learner variable. You are further saying if V_Learner variable has a value of Kinesthetic, to perform some kind of action. Let's program the action.

DISABLE PLAYBAR

Hiding the playbar using the Skin Editor disables it for the entire module. An alternative is disabling the playbar on the first slide only and locking the table of contents on the first slide. You will learn in the next scenario how to lock the table of contents and disable the playbar using the new actions loaded in Captivate 8.

RESOURCES

Working Sample: www.elearnvisual.com/advanced-interactions.html

Captivate source file: www.elearnvisual.com/members.html

(Enter the above URL in your Web browser.)

SCENARIO 5 - A Personalized and Customized Course Based from a Pretest (*Using Conditional Actions with User Variables and Quiz settings*)

PLEASE NOTE

Please note that there is an updated and quicker method of achieving this scenario with the use of **Pretest Questions**. Please see the topic **Using Pretest Questions**. The method in this chapter is presented for your practice in using variables and advanced actions.

SCENARIO

You would like your courses to have that personal touch for the user. Occasionally, you would like to address the user by first name. You would also like to customize the content and presentation of the course based on a user's prerequisite knowledge. Users of your course on **Microsoft Word 2007** are required to have taken the lesson: **Formatting Text** or possess the equivalent knowledge of Formatting Text before taking the advanced lesson, **Using Macros**. You would like to use a Pretest to determine if users should take the basics or advanced course. If users pass the pretest, they will be taken to the section of your course with **advanced** content. If they fail the pretest, they will be taken to the section of your course with **The Basics** content. Your navigation bar is disabled and table of contents (TOC) locked on all pretest slides, so that the user cannot skip the test.

THE SOLUTION:

Create user variables that store the participant's name. Add the new Captivate 8 actions to block navigation of the TOC and make the navigation bar invisible on pretest slides. Create in the **Quiz Preferences** an action for "If Passing Grade", jump to X slide and an action for "If Failing Grade" jump to Y slide, where X has advanced content and Y the Basics.

WHAT YOU WILL LEARN IN THIS TUTORIAL:

1. How to create user variables

2. How to configure system variables for controlling user navigation

3. How to use system variables to retrieve quiz scores.

3. How to configure Quiz preferences for pass/fail actions that utilize branching.

STEPS - 8 BASIC STEPS

1. Create an entry slide where you will collect user information

2. Insert a Text Entry Box and User variable to collect the user's name

3. Add Question slides with Pretest

4. Add extra Slides with Advanced and Basics content

5. Configure Pass/Fail actions for quiz to jump to slides with Advanced or Basics content

6. Configure system variables to block navigation of the TOC on Pretest slides

7. Add action to hide playbar on Pretest slides.

8. Use system variables to retrieve the user's quiz score.

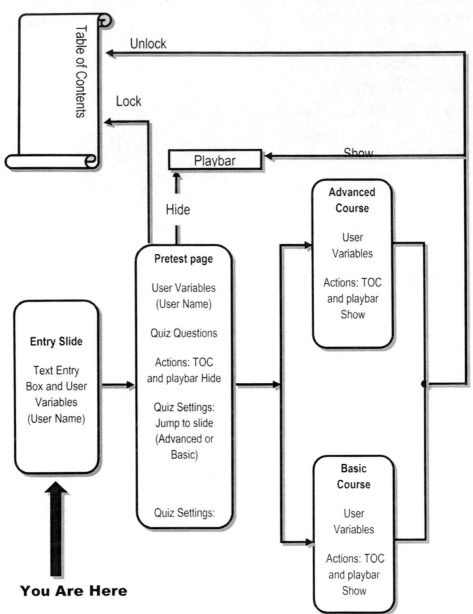

THE ENTRY SLIDE

LET'S LOOK AT THEM IN MORE DETAIL
THE ENTRY SLIDE

1

Create an **entry slide** where you will collect user information.

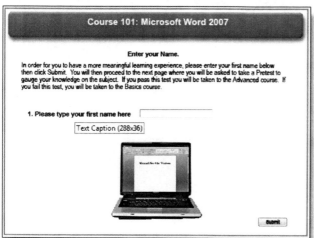

2

Insert a **Text Entry Box** and **User Variable** to collect the user's name.

2A

Click **Insert > Standard Objects > Text Entry Box**.
We will use it to collect the user's first name.

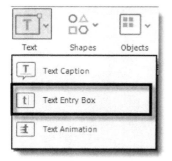

2B

De-select: **Retain Text, Validate User Input.**

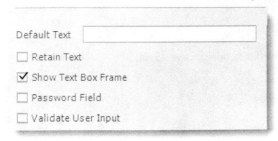

2C

In the **Action** area set: **On Success** - Go to next slide, **Attempts** - Infinite

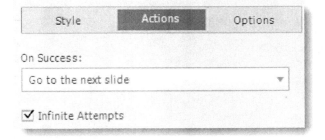

2D

In the **Display** section, check: **Hint.** In the **Others** section, check **Show button.**

2E

With the Text Entry Box selected, type a **name** for the variable to associate with the text entry box. We'll call it **V_Name_Pretest**

2F

Change the button type to Text button with text SUBMIT. The user will click this button after entering name.

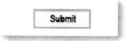

3

Text Add **extra Slides** for feedback texts and custom courses. This course will use branching scenarios - a path of slides for a **passing score** and a path of slides for a **failing score**.

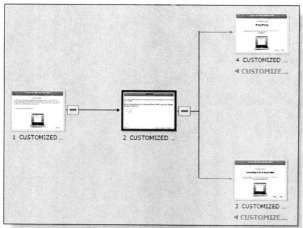

For this tutorial, we will create just 2 extra slides, one for a passing score and one for a failing score. Just remember, if in reality we are going to build a course of this complexity, it will consist of many slides, a group for a passing score and a group for a fail score.

THE CONTENT SLIDES:

1. A landing page if users pass the Pretest. This page will serve as the portal to the advanced course.

2. A landing page if users fail the Pretest. This page will serve as the portal to the Basics course.

ADDING THE VARIABLES - USER VARIABLE

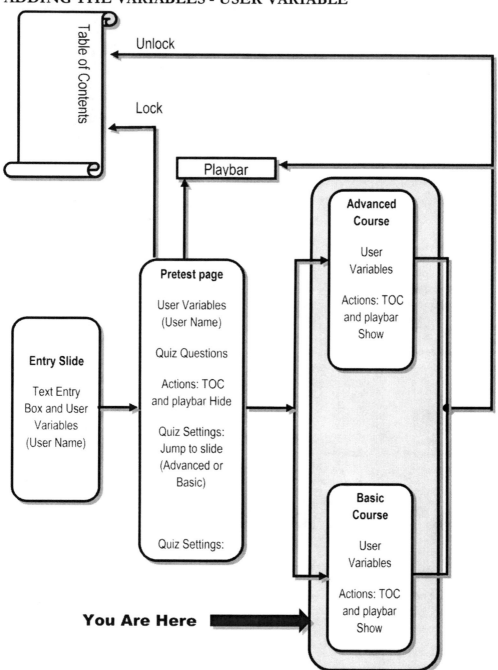

ADDING THE VARIABLES - USER VARIABLE

1

On the Advanced course landing page Insert a **Text Caption** with words that welcome the user and call the **V_Name_Pretest** user variable we created earlier.

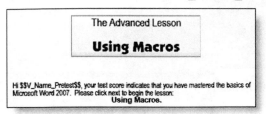

2

After typing "HI", Click the **Insert Variable icon** under the **Character** section of the Properties tab.

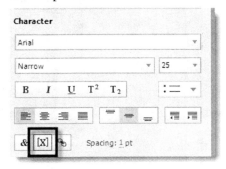

3

Under the **Variable Type** drop-down menu, select **User**.

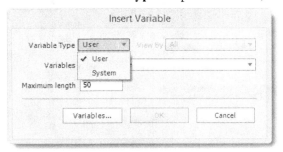

4

Under the **Variables** drop-down menu, select **V_Name_Pretest**

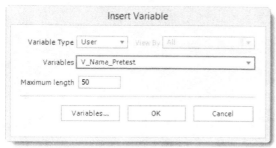

5

Click **OK**. Now the user will be addressed by their first name, wherever in the course you use the V_Name_Pretest variable.

SYSTEM VARIABLE

We use this variable to retrieve the user's quiz score after we have addressed the user by name.

1

In the text caption that uses the **V_Name_Pretest** variable, after

"Hi $$V_Name_Pretest$$, your test score of…"

Click the **Insert Variable icon** under the **Character** section of the Properties tab.

2

Under the **Variable Type** drop-down menu, select **System**.

3

Under the **View By** drop-down menu, select **Quizzing.**

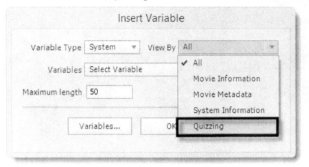

4

In the **Variables** drop-down menu, select **cpInfoPercentage**.

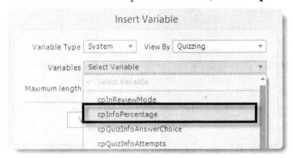

5

Click **OK**. Now the user will be addressed by their first name, and their score retrieved in this statement.

6

The script on the Advanced course landing page will look something like this:

*"Hi **$$V_Name_Pretest$$**, your test score of **$$cpInfoPercentage$$** indicates that you have mastered the basics of Microsoft Word 2007. Please click next to begin the lesson: **Using Macros**."*

Repeat the above steps for the basics course landing page so that the script looks like:

*Hi **$$V_Name_Pretest$$**, your test score of **$$cpInfoPercentage$$** indicates that you still need to master the basics of Microsoft Word 2007. Please click next to begin the lesson: **Formatting Text in Word 2007.***

QUIZ SETTINGS - THE QUESTION SLIDES:

1

Add the **question slides** that will serve as the Pretest.

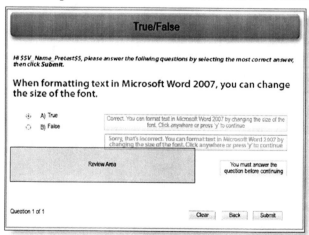

2

In the **Quiz** tab, set the questions **Type** as **Graded.**

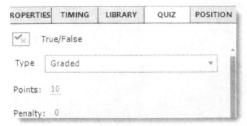

3

Check **Report Answers**.

4

Click **Quiz** > **Preferences** and set the **Pass/Fail Options**. For this tutorial, we have chosen **80%** as the passing grade.

5

Under the Actions section, set the Action for **On Success**. Configure it to **jump to slide** with Advanced content (Using Macros).

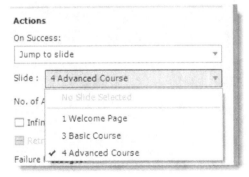

6

Set the Action for Failing Grade or **Last Attempt**. Configure it to jump to slide with The Basics content (**Formatting Text in Word 2007**).

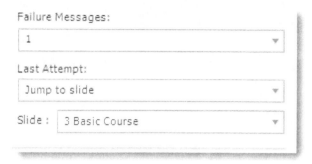

7

Ensure all other Quiz Preferences such as Correct Answers, Reporting, and Messages are configured as determined by your company's specifications.

HIDE & LOCK ACTIONS ON SLIDE ENTRY

1

Click the **Quiz slide**. In the Action panel of the Properties Inspector, Select **Execute Advanced Actions**.

2

Click the **Script** icon

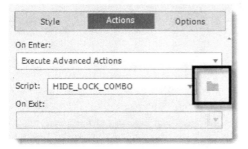

3

In the Advanced Actions dialog box click the plus **(+)** sign to create a new advanced action.

4

In the Action Type drop-down menu, select **Standard Actions**.

5

Click the **(+)** to add a new action to your advanced action.

6

Select the **action** you want performed. In this case, choose **Hide Playbar**.

7

Click the **(+)** to add a new action to your advanced action. This will add another action the line below your previous action.

8

Select the **action** you want performed. In this case, choose **Lock TOC**.

9

Name your Advanced Action.

NOTE: What you have just programmed is every time a user enters the quiz slide, hide the playbar and lock the table of contents.

Now for the landing pages with the Basic and Advanced courses, we are going to add advanced actions to unlock the table of contents that was locked in the Quiz slides and show the playbar that was hidden in the Quiz slides.

CONTROLLING USER NAVIGATION ON COURSE SLIDES
SHOW & UNLOCK ACTIONS ON SLIDE ENTRY

1

Click the **Basic Course slide**. In the Action area of the Properties panel, Select **Execute Advanced Actions.**

2

Click the **Script** icon.

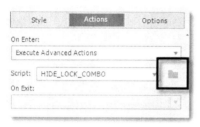

3

In the Advanced Actions dialog box click the plus (**+**) sign to create a new advanced action.

4

In the **Action Type** drop-down menu, select **Standard Actions**.

5

Click the (**+**) to add a new action to your advanced action.

6

Select the **action** you want performed. In this case, choose **Show Playbar**.

7

Click the **(+)** to add a new action to your advanced action. This will add another action the line below your previous action.

8

Select the **action** you want performed. In this case, choose **Unlock TOC**.

9

Name your Advanced Action.

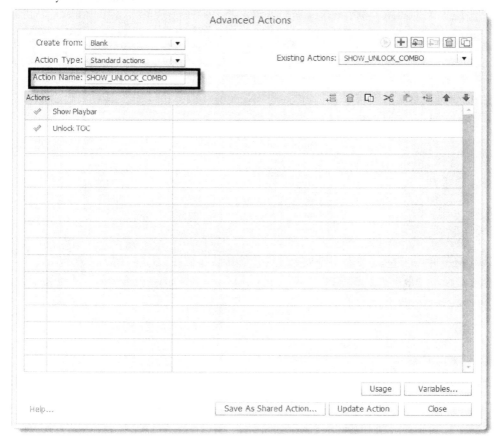

10

Click **Save / Update.**

11

Repeat the above steps for the **Advanced Course** landing slide.

> **NOTE**: What you have just programmed is every time a user enters the Basic Course landing slide., show the playbar and unlock the table of contents.

You may also want to consider disabling the playbar and locking the table of contents on the welcome slide. This will enforce that a user enters his or her name before proceeding.

RESOURCES

Working Sample: www.elearnvisual.com/advanced-interactions.html

Captivate source file: www.elearnvisual.com/members.html

(Enter the above URL in your Web browser.)

Creating & Using Shared Actions

One of the really nice features in Captivate 8 is that you can reuse advanced actions as Shared Actions in the same projects and across different projects.

Creating a Shared Advanced Action

1. To save your Advanced Action as a Shared Action, simply click the **Save as Shared Action** button in the Advanced Actions Scripting pane.

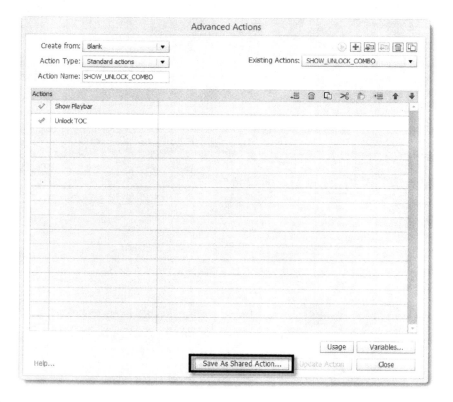

2. In the **Save As Shared Action** dialog box that launches, **Name** your Shared Action, add brief **descriptions** for the action and objects used. These descriptions will aid you when you have to reuse the action.

3. Click **Save** and **Close**.

Creating Advanced Actions From Shared Actions

1. To use a Shared Action as a template for building other Advanced Actions, click **Project > Advanced Actions.**

2. From the **Create from** drop-down list in the Advanced Actions dialog box, **select** one of the Shared Actions you created earlier that you would like to re-use.

3. Make any modifications to the Shared Action by adding new actions and parameters then click **Save As Action**. If there are many changes, you may want to save this as a new Shared Action by clicking **Save As Shared Action**.

Re–using Shared Actions in the same Project

Drag and Drop Shared Actions

To reuse a Shared Action you created earlier in the same project, simply drag the Shared Action from the library unto the object you want to apply the Shared Action like a button. You can then make any modifications if needed, in the window that launches.

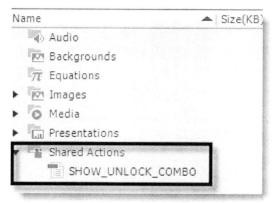

Using Shared Actions Across Different Projects

1. To share your Advanced Action across different projects, click the **Export** icon in the Advanced Actions dialog box.

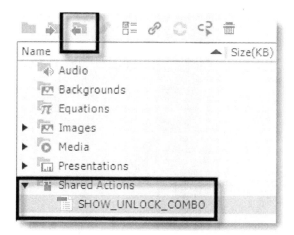

2. Give your Shared action a name and choose a location. Your shared action will **exported** in a **.cpaa** file extension.

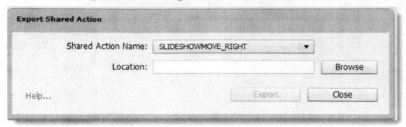

3. In the other project where you would like to reuse the Shared Action you just exported, click the **Import Icon** located in the Captivate Library or Advanced Actions dialog box.

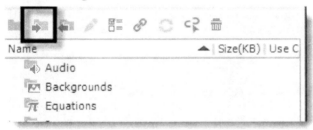

4. Navigate to where your .cpaa file is located and select it. Captivate inherits the Shared Action into the library and its now available for use in your current project.

9 – USING BEST PRACTICES
Achieving Consistency

1 – Use Templates

Having a style guide or template is essential for consistency in your project. Templates give all elements of your project a consistent and professional appearance, automates the design of new elements in your project, saving you lots of time and money from less rework. Templates will create standardized placeholders for different elements on your screens. Later, you can substitute those placeholders with your content. I highly recommend that your first step should be establishing how you want your project to look (size, color of elements, fonts, media etc.) then building templates around those specifications and have every designer in your project build their work from the templates.

Templates are especially important for very complex projects with several designers on a team, some of whom may be working remotely. When working on eLearning projects with many teams or with a huge design team, it is critical to balance creativity with consistency. Even if you are working alone on an eLearning project, with the flexibility to be creative, you should first decide on the details of how you want the course to look, and then build a template around those specifications. This template will be your style guide throughout the entire project. Since styles and tastes are subjective, if you leave it up to each designer in a team to choose what they want, you could end with an eLearning course with several different sizes of fonts for headings, different colors for the background, text captions designed differently for the same course and much more inconsistency. You would save yourself wasted efforts in rework and heartache later in your project, if you build your own templates.

2 – Use Master Slides

Use master slides to achieve consistency in the appearance of background graphics that remain constant throughout the project. Previously before their introduction, developers had to insert the background design slide by slide. Master slides function similar to master slides in PowerPoint. Changes in the master slide will be reflected in all the slides linked to it – a huge time saver. Master slides reduce development time significantly. You can also have more than one master slide linked to different dependent slides. Master slides are however, limited in controlling the styles of objects that may vary from screen to screen.

3 – Use Object Styles

Use **Object Styles** in Captivate 8 to achieve more consistency in the use of fonts throughout the project. Object Styles in Captivate 8 are similar to the styles feature of the other Adobe products like Dreamweaver, Photoshop, and Illustrator. Styles of objects can be saved as presets and reloaded when needed. If for example, you have decided that all H1 headings at the top of each screen should be in Arial font, size 28, then you can save this as a style with a name of your choice and load it each time you create an H1 heading. This not only results in shorter development time, but in more consistency. Time is money. A savings in time is a savings in money.

You can create object styles for:

Standard Objects:

- Captions
    - o Text Caption
    - o Rollover Caption
    - o Success Caption
    - o Failure Caption
    - o Hint Caption
- Text Entry Boxes
- Highlight Boxes
- Rollover Areas
- Rollover Slidelets
- Zoom Source and Destination
- Buttons
    - o Skip Button
    - o Back Button
    - o Continue Button
    - o Submit Button
    - o Clear Button
    - o Review Button
    - o Retake Button
- Progress Indicator
- Review Area

Quizzing Objects:

- Captions
- Correct Caption
- Incorrect Caption
- Retry Caption
- Timeout Caption
- Incomplete Caption
- Advanced Feedback Caption
- Title (Question/Result)
- Question Text
- Answers/FIB Text
- Header (Matching/Likert)
- Matching Entries
- Likert Question
- Scoring Result

4 – Use a Combination of Themes, Master Slides, Object Styles, and Placeholders in a Template

As mentioned previously, Captivate 8 offers some exciting tools for keeping a consistent look in your Captivate project. Use Themes to apply designs to your entire project with just one click of the mouse. Captivate 8 now has 11 enhanced themes with 20 preset sets of colors. You can further customize these colors allowing for many variations in the theme colors..

The combination of themes, master slides, object styles and placeholders in a template file provide more powerful tools for achieving consistency than previous versions of Captivate

If all developers and designers in a project build content using the same template, a high degree of consistency is achieved. This is critical for huge projects with several developers and designers working on different modules of a course.

5 – Use the Alignment Tools

Use the alignment tools to position objects in the exact position desired, to line objects completely justified to the left, right and so on. Using the alignment tools in Captivate you can achieve consistency by having text and graphics all aligned exactly left, right, top or bottom and distributed evenly. To enable the alignment tool bar, click **Window** > **Align**

6 – Use Position and Size Coordinates

You can also use the coordinate numbers: X Axis (**X**) and Y Axis (**Y**) Width (**W**) and Height (**H**) to provide consistency in the dimensions and positions of objects. All objects on a Captivate stage have (X) and (Y) coordinate values. A (**Y**) coordinate value determines the **vertical** position of an object and the (**X**) value the **horizontal**. So if for example you positioned a text box on the screen with an (X) value of 252 and (Y) value of 54, you can position that text box on another slide in the exact position using these numbers. These tools are located in the **Transform** tab of the Properties Inspector.

7 – Use Lock Size and Position of Objects

In previous versions of Captivate, when you locked an object not only did you lock its position, but you could not edit its properties. In Captivate 8 there is another option where you can just lock the size and position of an object and still be able to edit it. This is a great feature for objects that you do not want to accidentally move and continue working on them.

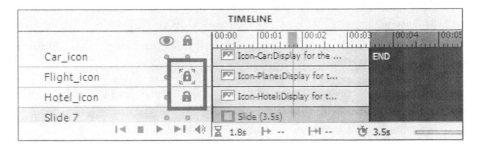

8 – Use Smart Positioning of Objects

The Smart Position feature assists you in achieving consistency in the positioning of objects across the project and display on mobile devices.

9 – Use Hexadecimal Numbers

Use hexadecimal numbers to create the exact colors you need for a project. This removes guesswork and provides consistency in choice of colors. Choice of colors can be tricky when left to an eye judgment. There are many shades of colors. To avoid using different shades of blue for hyperlinks for example, you can determine beforehand the shade of blue needed for hyperlinks, find out its hexadecimal value (Captivate gives the hexadecimal value for each color in the color palette), take a note of it, and use that value to create the right color for other hyperlinks in the rest of the project. A hexadecimal value for a shade of blue can look like #006EFF.

10 – Use the Eye Dropper Tool

Use the eye dropper tool to quickly choose the color of an object that is the same as another. This is a very quick way of sampling the same color of another object without using hexadecimal numbers. Using hexadecimal numbers is more accurate than this method.

Limiting Rework

11 – Use Spell Check

Use the Spell Check feature in Captivate immediately before publishing any project. It usually reveals a few typographical errors which the eye can overlook. This will limit editing and rework later.

12 – Use Copy / Paste

Use copy/paste to reduce rework. The copy/paste action is a huge time saver and limits the work of rebuilding things in Captivate, if used wisely. It is sometimes easier to copy/paste an object that took considerable time to construct, then editing what was pasted, instead of rebuilding everything from scratch. Here are a few items where copy/pasting can reduce rework.

- Objects in a template
- Rollover Slidelets
- Rollover Captions
- Question Pools
- Master slides
- Grouped Objects

The copy/paste function even works successfully from one Captivate 8 project to another.

Time-Saving Tips

13 – Use Template Objects

Use a pre-built template to save you time of rebuilding objects in Captivate projects. As mentioned before, you can copy/paste items from your template into your new project. This action works fine in Captivate 8 projects as the pasted items retain their original properties. Pasting from a Captivate 4 to Captivate 8 project may not work. Ensure that you copy from a Captivate 8 template to a Captivate 8 new project. I have also found it helpful to save the template under the name of the project you intend develop e.g. "Logging into The System." Your new project now has all the settings and properties of the template and you can now begin to build new slides, hide the template slides, copy/paste as needed.

14 – Use PowerPoint

Use PowerPoint source files to reduce development time in Captivate. Captivate 8 allow you not only to import PowerPoint presentations but also to edit those presentations inside Captivate. If you first develop as much content as you can in PowerPoint, then conduct a PowerPoint import into Captivate, You reduce development time significantly. Every time you add an object to a Captivate slide, such as text and images, they must be positioned and configured in a timeline. Sometimes these objects become out of sync with each other on the timeline and their timing must be manually synchronized. Configuring things in Captivate's timeline is time consuming. These timeline tasks are absent in PowerPoint projects and so you can simplify your development process by first building as much content as you can in PowerPoint, import into Captivate, then add quizzes, demos and interactivity if needed. This is especially helpful for developers who are new users to Captivate.

15 – Use Perpetual Buttons

By adding one instance of a **Smart Shape Perpetual Button** on a master slide, you can have navigation buttons automatically appear on every page – a huge time saver.

16 – Use Keyboard Shortcuts

Use keyboard shortcuts to simplify and reduce the time for repetitive tasks while working in Captivate. Here are some handy ones:

Copy – Control + C (Select the object. Press down the **Control** key while simultaneously pressing the **C** key)

Paste – Control + V

Cut – Control + X

Duplicate – Control + D

Undo – Control + Z

Select All Items in a List – Select first item + Shift + Select last item

In addition, Captivate usually has the shortcut keys listed for each task in the menu window that pops up. For example, click **Insert** and navigate down to **Image**, you will see the shortcut on the right for inserting an image which is: **Shift + Control + M**.

17 – Use "Sync with Playhead"

Use "Sync with Playhead" feature to quickly position objects on the timeline. As mentioned before, every time you insert an object into a slide, Captivate places it somewhere in the timeline. This automated action by Captivate is not perfect and developers usually have to synchronize things in the timeline, especially if there is audio. For example, you may want the "log in" text to appear only when "log in" is mentioned in the audio. Play the audio on the slide and when the playhead reaches the word "log in" in the audio, pause the audio, right click on the text object in the timeline and choose "Sync with Playhead."

18 – Use "Display for Rest of Slide"

Use "Display for Rest of Slide" to quickly set objects in the timeline. Right-click on an object in the timeline and choose "Display for rest of Slide" to quickly configure its timing to the timing of the entire slide. This is a lot quicker than dragging the tail end of the object to the end of the timeline. This feature is especially helpful when there is audio in the slide, making the timing of the slide up to 15 seconds or more.

19 – Use "Display for Rest of Project"

Use the "Display for Rest of Project" setting to save development time. Developers who use this setting appropriately save the time of individually pasting the same of object on each slide. It is especially suited for objects that will remain constant throughout the project. Here are a few examples where a "Display for Rest of Project" setting is ideal. In the cases below, place the items on the first slide only:

- Perpetual Buttons
- Standard Buttons where there is not much variation in the content
- Slide count variable
- Course name variable
- Project name variable
- Slide label variable

20 – Use Extra Screenshots When Recording Screens

Take extra screenshots when recording screens for a demonstration or simulation. This can save you the time and rework of recording screens again in case some screens in the recording were not clear enough. Sometimes glitches occur when recording screens with Captivate. Some screenshots are sometimes a little distorted or cropped in the wrong place or did not satisfy client requirements. Capturing extra screenshots with the **PrintScreen** keyboard button acts a backup.

21 – Use Variables To Automatically Add Topics to Slides

Use variables to quickly add topics to the top of slides without having type it for each slide. Place a **slide label variable ($$cpInfoCurrentSlideLabel$$)** on the first slide of the project. Place the variable at the top of the slide where you would like the topic to appear. Use the size, type and color of font on the variable that you would like for the topic and set the **Timing** to **"Display for Rest of Project"** setting. Label each slide with the appropriate topic. The topic for each slide will automatically appear at the top where you positioned the variable with the characteristics of the font you chose. You have just saved considerable time from manually entering the topic for each slide. Remember also that the **table of contents** pulls information from the slide labels, so labeling your slides is always a best practice.

Another alternative to automatically add slide topics using variables is to put the slide label variable (**$$cpInfoCurrentSlideLabel$$**) on a **master slide**. Like in the example above, place the variable in the same position on the master slide where you would like the topics to appear for each slide. All slides linked to that master slide will automatically have the topic displayed.

22 – Use Variables to Automatically Number Slides

Use variables to quickly add slide numbers to every slide that can look like – Slide 1 of 35. As in the previous example, place the variable (**Slide $$cpInfoCurrentSlide$$ of $$rdinfoSlideCount$$**) on the first slide in the position where you would like the slide count to appear. Ensure that the variable has the font type, size and color that you want for the slide count and set its timing to "**Display for Rest of Project**".

23 – Use Find and Replace

Use **Find and replace** to quickly make edits to Captivate projects. For example, you can quickly change all instances of "LMS" to "Learning Management System" by simply using the Find and Replace feature in Captivate. Click **Edit > Find and Replace**. In the **Find** field enter the word you would like to replace which in this case is "LMS." In the **Replace** field enter the corrected word which in this case is "Learning Management System." Click **Find Next** and **Replace** repeatedly till you have corrected all occurrences of "LMS." You can also click **Find All** and **Replace All** to quickly make all corrections.

24 – Use Text-to-Speech Vs Recording

Use the text-to-speech feature to quickly add audio to slides when there are time, money, equipment, and voice over talent limitations. To add audio to a slide using the text-to-speech feature can be done in as quickly a time as 5 minutes. Using voice over talent requires time to set up the appointment with the narrator, time to do the actual recording, time to clean the audio after the recording and time to insert it into Captivate after cleaning. Using the text-to-speech feature is a huge time-saver, but you must use professional voices to achieve professional results.

You may be surprised to know the pleasant results you can achieve using this technology. It is not only faster and cheaper than hiring narration talent but can sometimes be advantageous. When development of e-learning has many iterations and changes, edits to the content including the audio can easily be made without having to go back to a recording studio, re-recording or rehiring voice-over talent.

Gone are the days when TTS technology had a very robotic sound like Microsoft's first generation voices. AT&T Natural Voices, Neospeech, Acapela, Cepstral Voices and Ivona have produced some very realistic sounding TTS voices.

Suggested Voices for Text-to-Speech

"Voices" are the files that provide the information for conversion of the text to audio. They must be installed on your computer for the conversion to occur. The text-to-speech feature is upgraded in Captivate 8 to include 4 more voices. Captivate 8 will also load all voices installed in your system in addition to the ones shipped with the software. Here are some realistic sounding voices that you can purchase:

IVONA - Eric, Jennifer, Kendra, Joey, Kimberly, Salli (Teenage), Ivy (Child), Brian (UK), Emma (UK)

(#1 Recommendation)

Neospeech – Kate (Included in Captivate 8 - You may need to download it separately), Paul (Included in Captivate 8), Charles (UK), Audrey (UK)

AT&T Natural Voices – Mike, Rich, Crystal, Alberto and Rosa (Spanish)

Acapela Group – Aaron, Heather, Laura, Ryan, Graham (UK), Lucy (UK)

Cepstral – Allison, David, Diane, William, Lawrence (UK), Millie (UK)

Improving the Quality of Text-to-Speech

1. Audio Bitrates

Encode all audio mp3 files in the project at a bitrate of no less than 128 kilobits per second (kbps).

Click **Audio > Settings** and choose **CD Bitrate (128 kbps)**.

Although this will increase the file size somewhat, it's better to have clean sounding audio at the expense of a slight increase in file size than to have a small file hosting poor quality audio. Audio mp3 files encoded at 128 kbps is near CD quality and is the lowest standard used for online music stores such as iTunes and Rhapsody.

2. Use High Quality SAPI5 Voices Encoded at 16 KHz

The **Speech Application Programming Interface (SAPI)** is an API developed by Microsoft to allow the use of speech recognition and speech synthesis within Windows applications. Earlier text-to-speech technology used SAPI1 through 4 voices such as Microsoft Mary, Mike and Sam. These had a very robotic sound. With the introduction of SAPI5, the quality of the voices has improved significantly. SAPI5 voices were first released in 2000.

Ensure that you are using SAPI5 voices. The ones listed previously are excellent choices.

The IVONA voices are amazingly clean and of a high quality. Remember that audio encoded at 16 KHz is of a higher quality than audio at 8 kHz. For professional purposes, ensure that you are using the 16 kHz voices. Telephone speech is usually encoded at 64Kbs at a sampling rate of 8 KHz. 16 KHz voices are recommended for eLearning material that will be hosted on a web server, LMS or Disc.

3. Punctuation

Use punctuation such as commas, exclamation marks, question marks and periods in convenient places to aid in readability and tone of the narration. Commas are especially important in text-to-speech work. You may need to add extra commas that were not in the original script to improve the flow of the narration.

4. VTML Tags

Use VTML (Voice Text Markup Language) tags to achieve powerful control of pitch, speed, volume, pauses and pronunciation of specific sections and words of the narration.

Using this powerful hidden gem in text-to-speech projects helps you control the generated speech and improve its tonal quality.

Pitch

This value defines the pitch of the synthesized voice. A pitch with a value of 100(%) is normal. The possible pitch range is 50- 200(%). The higher the pitch value, the higher the pitch.

Example:

<vtml_pitch value="120">_Your Text_**</vtml_pitch>**

Pronunciation

Use an alias to help in the pronunciation of a word when the TTS engine is not doing a good job.

Example:

<vtml_sub alias="Jim">_Gym_**</vtml_sub>**

To pronounce "Gym" as "Jim."

Speed

This value defines the speed of the synthesized voice. A speed with a value of 100(%) is normal. The possible speed range is 50 - 400%. The higher the speed value, the higher the speed.

Example:

<vtml_speed value="80">Your Text**</vtml_speed>**

Volume

This value defines the speed of the synthesized voice. A speed with a value of 100(%) is normal. The possible speed range is 0 - 500%. The higher the volume value, the louder the volume.

Example:

<vtml_volume value="150">Your Text**</vtml_volume>**

Pause

This value defines the length of pause of the synthesized voice. A pause with a value of 687(msec) is normal. The range is 0 - 65535(msec). The higher the pause value, the longer the pause.

Example:

Your**<vtml_pause time="80"/>**Text

Preventing Costly Blunders

25 – Use Version File Names

Save major updates to a Captivate project under a new version file name. This practice can save you the heartache of a Captivate file that has become corrupted and will not open. You can always revert to the last major version of the file. An example of this is saving the project under the name "accessing_the_lms_v1" after developing 5 slides. Then after 15 slides, save under "accessing_the_lms_v1b," after developing 25 slides, save under"accessing_the_lms_v1c," after adding quizzes, "accessing_the_lms_v1d" and so on. If "accessing_the_lms_v1d." becomes corrupt or messed up for some reason and is irrecoverable, all your work is not lost. You can open "accessing_the_lms_v1c" and resume developing with little rework.

26 – Use Regular Back Ups

Back up major updates to a Captivate project on both a shared drive and flash drive. As in the previous example, this practice can save you the agony of a project on which you have spent significant development hours, lost through an accidental deletion or corruption. Files can even be accidentally deleted on a shared drive. It is a good practice to back up your work on both a portable USB device and shared drive while working of your PC drive.

27 – Use Locks

Locking slides and specific objects in the timeline help prevent accidentally messing up elements that you have already built. This is a very good practice and will save you the blunder of accidentally changing objects you have already configured and hours of rework. Locking objects in the timeline is especially helpful when you are working on objects that are in close proximity to each other or that may overlap each other on the screen.

28 – Use Show/Hide

Use the Show/Hide icon to aid in developing on a screen with many objects. Each object on the screen is represented in the timeline with an eye icon next to the lock icon. When there are many objects on a screen, for example, several images, with several text captions and rollover captions, it is good practice to use the Show/Hide icon to make every other objects temporarily invisible except the one on which you are working. This allows you to focus on one object at a time, avoids confusion and accidentally messing up other objects.

29 – Use Slide Numbers Below 100

Use below 100 slides in a project to get optimum performance from Captivate. The software is known to have issues in huge projects that exceed 100 slides. Such projects are more prone to crashes, erratic behavior, corrupted slides and bugs displaying themselves.

Achieving High Quality

30 – Record Audio Outside Captivate

Use software outside Captivate to achieve the highest audio quality rather than recording audio with the Captivate software. You will achieve far better audio quality and stability by using **Adobe Audition,** a part of the Adobe eLearning Suite. Audition also has excellent tools for cropping the audio and removing background noise. You can also use excellent free software like **Audacity,** which you can download from the Internet. After recording and cleaning your audio outside of Captivate, then perform an import into Captivate.

31 – Optimize Image Quality

Use high resolution images in your Captivate projects. Pixilated and blurry images always look unprofessional in an eLearning project. In spite of how great the content may be, blurry images will make your entire project appear unprofessional. Use images with a **PNG** (Portable Network Graphics) file extension rather than JPEGS (Joint Photographic Experts Group). JPEGS are a compressed format and loses image quality the higher the compression. PNG files are also better because they can carry transparency qualities while JPEGS cannot. Ensure the images are of a resolution of no less than 100 dpi (dots per inch).

If your project has many images with a **PNG** extension, ensure that you select **Optimized** or **High (24bit)** in the Quality drop-down menu of the Properties Inspector.

32 – Clean the Library

Keeping the library as clean as possible will keep the size of the published files as small as possible and improve playback of the material on an LMS or Web server. Captivate will keep unused items in the library even if you deleted those items from the slides. Before publishing, click the Library tab and click the **Select Unused Items** icon that looks like a broken chain link. Captivate will then highlight all the unused items in the project. Click the adjacent **Delete** icon. All unused items will be deleted. This one action can reduce your published file size by as much as 50%.

Conclusion

Many of the above best practices I have acquired through my own experience working with Captivate and following industry standards for multimedia and artistic work. As you build experience in Adobe Captivate, you will develop your own best practices. My hope is that you can supplement the new ones you have learned in this material with the ones you already have. Many of the above best practices can be transferred to other eLearning and multimedia software. Happy experiences in Captivate developing.

10 – USING ADVANCED QUIZZING

Using Question Pools

Sometimes to avoid the predictability in quizzes, an organization may decide to use **random questions** that can be presented to the users in any order and from a pool of questions. To create random questions we must first create a **Question Pool**.

Creating a Question Pool

1. In your Captivate project, click **Quiz > Question Pool Manager**.

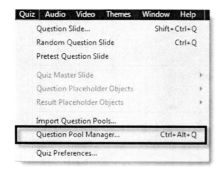

2. The **Question Pool Manager** launches.

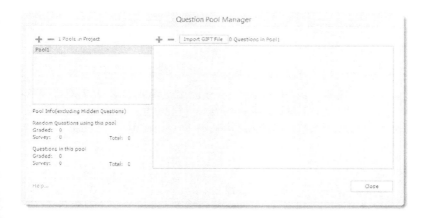

3. To add a Question Pool, Click the **plus (+)** symbol above the left pane.

4. Give the Question Pool a **name** of your choice. No spaces are allowed in the name.

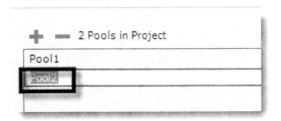

5. With the new question pool selected, **click** the Questions **plus symbol (+)**

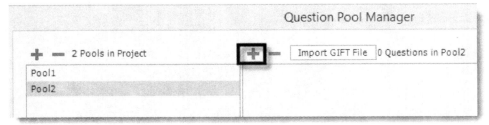

You can also import questions into the pool by clicking the **Import GIFT File** button. A GIFT (General Import Format Technology) is a text file format of the quiz questions that is used in Learning Management Systems like Moodle.

6. From the Insert Questions dialog box, select the type of questions, and for each question the quantity and whether Graded or Survey.

7. Click OK.

8. The new questions are listed in the Question Pool Manager and added to the Question Pool. Use the Question Pool Manager to add additional questions to a pool.

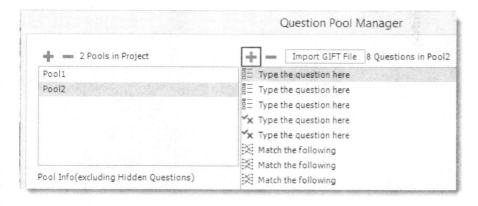

9. Close the Question Pool Manager and click **Window** > **Question Pool** to launch the Question Pool Tab with the questions under each pool. Drag the **Question Pool Tab** to your desired location.

10. Under the Question Pool Tab, **click each question** to **edit** its **properties** in the **Quiz** tab of the Property Inspector.

Using Random Questions

1. After creating one or more Question Pools, navigate to the Filmstrip panel and **click the slide** after which you want to insert a random question.

2. Click **Quiz > Random Question Slide**

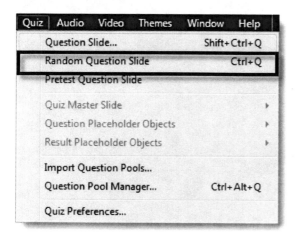

3. A Random Question Slide is added to the project.

4. **Click** the Random Question Slide and in the Quiz Panel **select** the **Question Pool** to which you would like to **link** the Random Question.

Captivate 8 will program random questions to be presented to the user from the pool you selected.

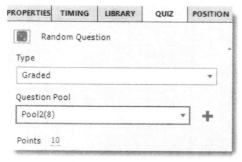

5. Select the **Actions** for your Random Question.

Using Pretest Questions with Branching

Pretest questions facilitate testing a user's knowledge of basic information prior to completing a course. There are several situations where pretest questions are ideal. Here are a few.

- A pretest/post-test study to measure learning

- To qualify users with prior knowledge of the material by quickly completing the pretest and moving on to the advanced course, after passing. Those who fail the pretest will be directed to the basic course.

- To provide trainers with a means of measuring prior knowledge of the material.

To insert a pretest question into your project:

1. Click **Quiz > Question Slide**.

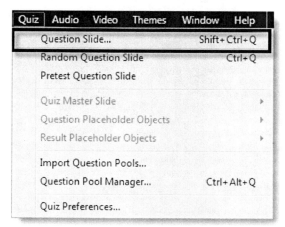

2. In the **Insert Questions** dialog box, specify the type and amount of questions. For each question, click the drop-down menu on the right and select **Pretest**.

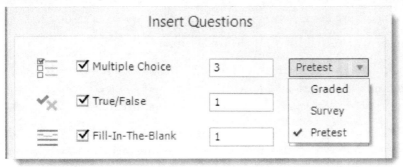

3. Click one of the Pretest questions on the filmstrip

4. Click the **Quiz** tab in the Properties panel.

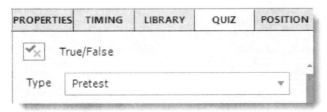

5. Click **Edit Pretest Action** in the **Action** section of the Properties panel.

Actions

No. of Attempts: 1

☐ Infinite Attempts

☐ Retry Message

Failure Messages:

None

Edit Pretest Action

6. The Advanced Actions script editor launches. By default, the Pretest Advanced action (**CpPrestestAction**) is added and uses the **cpQuizInfoPretestScorePercentage** system variable. We are going to edit this Advanced action for our project. Remember that **Conditional Advanced actions** consist of three sections: IF, ACTION and ELSE sections. We will edit each section.

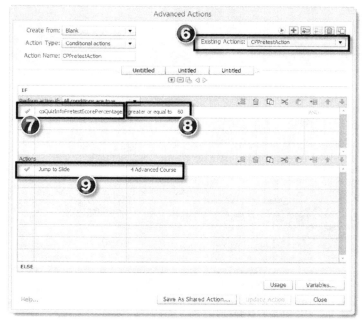

7. In the **IF** section of the Script editor, if you have chosen points instead of percentage as the quiz score in the quiz settings, double-click the variable name and choose **cpQuizInfoPretestPointScored**. For our project, we will leave it as **cpQuizInfoPretestScorePercentage**.

8. Let us change the passing percentage in the **IF** section. Double-click **is greater than** and select **is greater or equal to**. Double-click the value after **is greater or equal to** and change it from **50** to **literal 80**.

9. In the **Actions** section of the Script Editor, the default action is Go to Next Slide. We need to change that to the slide where our Advanced Course begins. Double-click **Go to Next Slide** and select the **Jump to Slide** action and specify the specific slide where the **Advanced Course** begins.

What we have just programmed is if the user obtains a percentage that is greater or equal to 80%, jump to slide 5, where the advanced course begins.

10. Click the **ELSE** section of the Script editor and edit the default action from **Next Slide** to **Jump to Slide**. Then select the specific slide where the **Basic Course** is located.

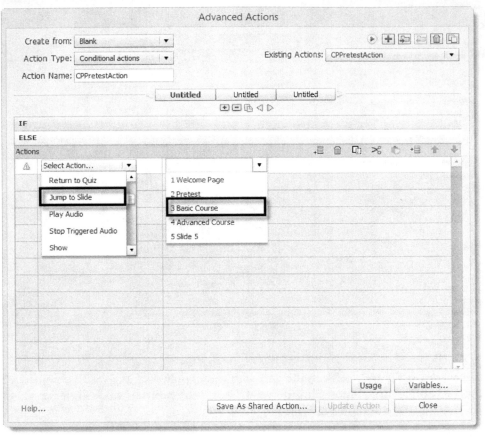

11. What you have just programmed is:

IF: the user obtains a percentage that is greater or equal to 80% on the Pretest,

ACTION: jump to the slide, where the Advanced Course begins.

ELSE: jump to the slide, where the Basic Course is begins.

Your edited Pretest Advanced actions should look like the following screenshots.

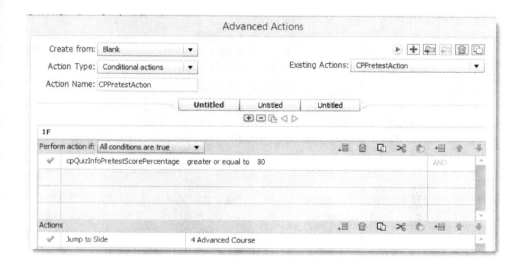

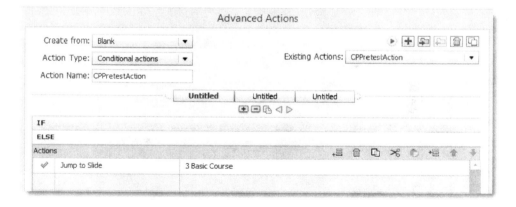

Index

About the Author

Wayne Pascall is a Captivate developer, instructional technologist, artist, and author. Wayne also uses his skills as a fine artist to design and prepare graphics for eLearning courses. As a fine artist he specializes in pencil drawings, digital art, acrylic and oil paintings.

Artist Gallery:

http://wayne-pascall.artistwebsites.com

CPSIA information can be obtained at www.ICGtesting.com
Printed in the USA
BVOW04s2201010215

385949BV00007B/75/P